OUTSOURCING NATIONAL DEFENSE

Outsourcing National Defense

Why and How Private Contractors Are Providing Public Services

Thomas C. Bruneau

LYNNE RIENNER PUBLISHERS

BOULDER
LONDON

Published in the United States of America in 2023 by
Lynne Rienner Publishers, Inc.
1800 30th Street, Suite 314, Boulder, Colorado 80301
www.rienner.com

and in the United Kingdom by
Lynne Rienner Publishers, Inc.
Gray's Inn House, 127 Clerkenwell Road, London EC1 5DB
www.eurospanbookstore.com/rienner

© 2023 by Lynne Rienner Publishers, Inc. All rights reserved

Library of Congress Cataloging-in-Publication Data
Names: Bruneau, Thomas C., author.
Title: Outsourcing national defense : why and how private contractors are
   providing public services / Thomas C. Bruneau.
Description: Boulder, Colorado : Lynne Rienner Publishers, Inc., [2023] |
   Includes bibliographical references and index. | Summary: "An in-depth
   investigation of the scope, legality, and implications of the US private
   sector's vast involvement in securing the nation"— Provided by
   publisher.
Identifiers: LCCN 2022037650 (print) | LCCN 2022037651 (ebook) | ISBN
   9781955055925 (hardcover) | ISBN 9781955055956 (ebook)
Subjects: LCSH: United States. Department of Defense—Officials and
   employees. | Defense industries—United States. | Contracting
   out—United States. | Privatization—United States. | Civil-military
   relations—United States. | United States—Military policy. | Private
   military companies—United States—History.
Classification: LCC UA23 .B78464 2023 (print) | LCC UA23 (ebook) | DDC
   355.6/2120973—dc23/eng/20220830
LC record available at https://lccn.loc.gov/2022037650
LC ebook record available at https://lccn.loc.gov/2022037651

British Cataloguing in Publication Data
A Cataloguing in Publication record for this book
is available from the British Library.

Printed and bound in the United States of America

The paper used in this publication meets the requirements
of the American National Standard for Permanence of
Paper for Printed Library Materials Z39.48-1992.

5 4 3 2 1

I dedicate this book to my wife, Celia, whose courage in the face of serious medical challenges gave me daily inspiration during the four years it took to research and write it.

Contents

Preface ix

1 Outsourcing National Defense 1
2 The Historical and Legal Context 19
3 Supporting the Global War on Terrorism 31
4 Contracting Out Intelligence 61
5 Facing Great Power Competition 81
6 Developing Advanced Technologies 101
7 Public Money, Private Gains 133

List of Acronyms 143
Bibliography 145
Index 161
About the Book 167

Preface

I BECAME AWARE OF THE OUTSOURCING OF SERVICES BY THE DEPARTment of Defense (DoD) in the 1990s, when I was a professor at the Naval Postgraduate School (NPS), which is part of DoD. At that time, custodial and landscaping services were contracted out. Looking into what I considered unacceptable performance, I learned that contractor employees did not report to anybody at NPS, but rather only to the firm that was awarded the contract. Later, as chairman of the National Security Affairs Department and then director of the Center for Civil-Military Relations at NPS, I learned how to write contracts and to oversee contractors in order to ensure accountability and acceptable performance.

On retiring, I founded a contracting firm, Global Academic Professionals. While I was awarded some contracts, I soon learned that there is much more to success in winning contracts than knowledge and competence. The process and authorities—in short, the acquisition framework based on the Federal Acquisition Regulation (FAR)—and even personal contacts proved to be critically important.

After following and publishing on the topic of DoD contracting out from the beginning of the global war on terrorism in 2001 to the present, I undertook a new research project to better understand the larger domain of contracting out by DoD (beyond private security contractors). This book, the culmination of my work on civil-military relations and the outsourcing of security, is the outcome of that project.

* * *

To adequately acknowledge the support and contributions I received over the thirty years or so while I developed the ideas and obtained the information for this book is impossible.

I owe many debts, both intellectual and information based. To Jim Schweiter, I am grateful for the invaluable insights he gave me based upon his decades-long work in the US Congress, at DoD, and in "the industry" of contracting out. Over the years, I have learned from the officer students and faculty in the Acquisition Management Curriculum at NPS. Bernard Martin, a long-time high-level staffer at the Office of Management and Budget, put me in touch with Alan Burman, the administrator of the Office of Federal Procurement Policy during the period when the A-76 process, and inherently governmental functions, were being defined by his office. My congressman, Jimmy Panetta, was instrumental in putting me in touch with research staff in the Congressional Research Service and Government Accountability Office, which facilitated my receiving timely and objective information on several of the issues covered in the pages that follow.

I learned about Other Transaction Authority (OTA) from undoubtedly the major expert in the field, Richard L. Dunn of the Strategic Institute FOR Innovation in Government Contracting. In addition to his invaluable podcasts, he was also willing to respond to my frequent, often poorly informed queries on the nature and use of OTAs. He also provided me with case studies on the use of OTAs. Megen Schlesinger of the Naval Postgraduate School's Emerging Technology Consortium first interested me in the use of OTAs, and Secretary of the Navy Richard V. Spencer drew my attention in 2018 to the need for DoD to draw upon the technological innovations emerging from Silicon Valley.

It was my position as rapporteur of the Defense Policy Board (1998–2001) with William Cohen, then secretary of defense, and Brent Scowcroft, then chairman of the board, as well as other luminaries including Richard Crowe and Andrew Marshall, that drew my attention to the centrality of both the Department of Defense and the US Congress in all that concerns national security and defense, both governmental and outsourced. The respect that I gained for the secretary of defense and his tremendous responsibilities in charge of the largest and most complex organization in the world led me to draw heavily on books and articles by later secretaries of defense: Robert Gates, Ash Carter, and James Mattis.

I am overjoyed to publish once again with Lynne Rienner, with whom I have been working since even before she founded her own press. And I am grateful for the support of Marie-Claire Antoine, senior acquisitions editor at Lynne Rienner Publishers, throughout the process of developing the manuscript for this book.

1

Outsourcing National Defense

THE FISCAL YEAR 2020 BUDGET FOR THE US DEPARTMENT OF DEFENSE (DoD) was $738 billion. Of this sum, DoD obligated $420 billion in contracts, funding 464,500 full-time contract employees.[1] A data point to convey the scale of contracting-out is provided by the decision of the Biden administration to withdraw US troops from Afghanistan by September 11, 2021. Media reports at that time indicated there were between 2,500 and 3,500 US troops in Afghanistan. According to data in a Congressional Research Service report, in the fourth quarter of 2020 there were 22,562 contractors, 7,856 of them US citizens, employed by DoD in Afghanistan.[2] The anticipated heavy reliance on contractors, especially those maintaining airplanes and helicopters for Afghan pilots, has been indicated by some analysts as a reason why Afghanistan fell to the Taliban so quickly in early August 2021.[3] A telling statement on the centrality of contractors to US national security is the following by Matthieu Aikins: "The U.S. military had spent billions to train and equip a force in its own image, heavily dependent on foreign contractors and air support."[4] By virtue of the scale of funds involved, and the number of contracted employees, any effort to analyze US defense policy, including civil-military relations, must include outsourcing. It will become clear in the discussion of contingency contracting in the global war on terrorism and the current effort to obtain the latest technology to aid the warfighter in the great power competition that it is impossible today to implement a US defense strategy without a reliance on contractors.[5]

There is no contracting-out without the awarding of a contract.[6] And there are a huge number of contracts. Ash Carter, who had been, as he terms it in his book, "acquisition czar," then deputy secretary of defense, and then secretary of defense under President Obama, writes: "There are about ten million such separate contracts awarded each year [by DoD]."[7] The contracts transfer what I have heard congressmen refer to as "the people's money" to for-profit firms, called "the industry." Again, it should be no surprise that the transfer of the people's money to the industry is regulated by law, commonly called "authorities," which are found in the Code of Federal Regulations and United States Code. In this book, I focus first on the Federal Acquisition Regulation (FAR) (48 Code of Federal Regulations) and the DoD's Defense Federal Acquisition Regulation Supplement (DFARS), which is codified at Title 48 of the Code of Federal Regulations and Other Transaction Authority (OTA) (10 US Code 4021–4023).[8] It must be noted that there are three main dimensions—processes and structures—that directly impinge on outsourcing by DoD. The first is the budgeting system, the second is the definition of requirements, and the third is the awarding of contracts. As might be expected of anything as huge and complex as DoD, all three are very complicated, and it should be no surprise that the results are less than optimum. I have chosen to focus on the awarding of contracts in this book both because it is fundamental and also because the current system, based on the FAR, is being questioned not only by professional experts in outsourcing but also by the US Congress. Yet the adherence to the FAR by the contracting community is almost total, and based upon my research and personal experience over decades with contracting officers, I am convinced that the answer lies in the nature of incentives.

I have two goals in this book. First, to contribute to the conceptualization of civil-military relations by examining how the United States outsources to private, for-profit firms large elements of security, most of which previously had been a monopoly of the US government. Second, and in order to achieve that goal, I first explore how outsourcing works. To do so, I utilize a framework for analysis based on one we have formulated and used in the conceptualization of civil-military relations. While many of the books on one aspect of outsourcing—the privatization of security via private security contractors—tend to be polemical, this book assumes the position that outsourcing by DoD "is what it is." That is, it is a fact, it will not go away, and the scope and importance of this fact behooves us to understand it.

Framework for Analysis

Possibly due to the gigantic fiscal and personnel scale as well as the complexity and lack of reliable data on outsourcing security, there are, to the best of my knowledge, very few if any analytical books or articles on this topic. Nor is there any agreement on how to approach reform of the acquisition process, let alone what must be done to reform a system within which acquisition processes are central. As Ash Carter writes: "Unfortunately, pressures from well-intentioned but sometimes misguided defense experts, consultants, and members of Congress often drive the Pentagon's processes in the wrong direction. As a result, most of the periodic paroxysms of 'acquisition reform' that sweep through government have been amateurish and counterproductive. I know, because I've had a front-row seat for several of them."[9]

The title of probably the main book on acquisition reform is suggestive of the situation: *Defense Acquisition Reform, 1960–2009: An Elusive Goal*, by J. Ronald Fox. Another typical title on the same topic is: "We Are Lost in the Woods on Acquisition Reform."[10] Observers have identified cycles of acquisition reform, yet there is no consensus on whether the acquisition function is being reformed or not.[11] It is relevant to the focus in this book that the US Government Accountability Office (GAO) assesses DoD contract management, which includes operational contract support, as in global war on terrorism, as high-risk.[12]

The inspiration for my approach in this book is conveyed in a quote from John Lewis Gaddis's *On Grand Strategy:* "Because ends exist only in the imagination, they can be infinite: a throne on the moon, perhaps with a great view. Means, though, are stubbornly finite: they're boots on the ground, ships in the sea, and the bodies required to fill them. Ends and means have to connect if anything is to happen. They're never, however, interchangeable."[13] In short, strategy is the vision of matching ends with means, and in US national security a great many of the means are outsourced. While there is a huge literature on strategy, including "Grand Strategy," there is virtually nothing on the "means" whereby a strategy might be implemented.

The topic of outsourcing by DoD is amorphous. In order to identify and organize a gigantic quantity of data and documents of variable focus and reliability, I utilize and adapt a framework for analysis that was developed for the study of civil-military relations in which the traditional concept of civilian control over the armed forces was expanded to include the concept of military effectiveness.[14] The framework was developed from research in the United States and other countries, and it is based upon the requirements necessary for control and effectiveness, which include the legal basis for control, oversight mechanisms, and education of those responsible, strategy, institutions, and resources. These concepts were operationalized with a variety of data.

In adapting the framework to outsourcing, I use the components of the framework to identify and organize what I consider to be credible information. I thus propose the following components of the framework for this book. The legal bases for outsourcing are the Federal Acquisition Regulation and Other Transaction Authority. Oversight is ultimately with the US Congress and its research and analysis arms.[15] Education and training pertain to those responsible for implementing the legal bases for contracting out. In the case of the global war on terrorism, they include contracting officers (CO), contracting officer representatives (CORs), and officers who are not acquisition specialists; and for great power competition it is again contracting officers, but specifically in dealing with Other Transaction Authorities (OTAs), they may be termed agreement officers. The US national security strategies, the visions of matching ends with means, to be focused on are the global war on terrorism (between 2001 and 2018) and great power competition (2018–present).[16] The institutions are those that see to the implementation of the strategies to achieve their goals. For the global war on terrorism it is the COs and CORs, and in intelligence it is the Office of the Director of National Intelligence (ODNI). So far, as OTAs are a potential acquisition vehicle for technological innovations, but as argued below have yet to "catch on," there is no equivalent institution to see to implementation, although several have been proposed.[17] As noted earlier, in 2020, the US Department of Defense obligated $420 billion in contracts funding 464,500 full-time contract employees.[18] Lest one assume that these funds were mainly to purchase equipment—ships, planes, tanks, and the like—to be used by uniformed military personnel, the most recent available data show that 51 percent of total DoD contracts were for services, 41 percent for goods or equipment, and 8 percent for research and development (R&D).[19] In short, a minimum of 51 percent of these funds, and a maximum of 59 percent, were used to replace, support, or in some manner affect the military effectiveness of a uniformed personnel totaling 1.3 million active and 800,000 reserve forces.[20] Figure 1.1 provides both some insight into the amount of funds outsourced to services as well as the challenges arising from the lack of a single definition of services and the unreliability of the data. While the data reported at the outset of this chapter are from the Congressional Research Service (CRS), the data displayed here are from the GAO, both supporting the US Congress.

My attention was drawn to the centrality of the legal basis for outsourcing, the authorities in the global war on terrorism, under the FAR, on reading Secretary of Defense Robert M. Gates's *Duty: Memoirs of a Secretary at War*, wherein he states: "At the end of May, I approved putting the MRAP [mine-resistant, ambush-protected vehicles] program in a special, very small category of Defense procurement, effectively-setting aside many bureaucratic hurdles typical of military programs."[21] The bureaucratic hurdles referenced by the secretary of defense are also perceived to hamper outsourcing in the great power competition—resulting in recommendations to replace the FAR with the OTA as the legal framework, or authority, of choice. Who makes these recommendations will be discussed in Chapter 6.

I propose to use this adapted framework not only because there is no other available framework on this topic, but also because of the sheer complexity and scale in outsourcing, the ambiguity in definitions and data, and impediments to research. This framework allows me to identify relevant information and to analyze how it fits together as a whole.

Figure 1.1 Department of Defense Spending on Contractors, Fiscal Year 2020 (Billions of US$)

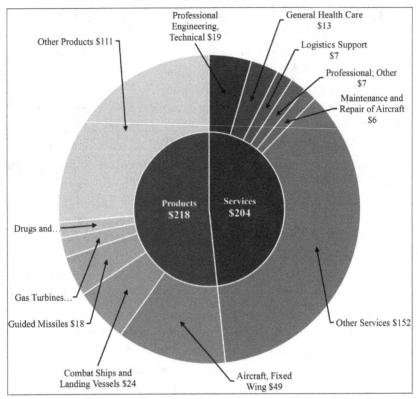

Source: GAO, https://www.gao.gov/blog/snapshot-goverment-wide-contracting-fy-2020-infographic.

Research Issues

The main impediments to research I encountered concerned first defining what constitutes a service and then the availability of data, including issues of secrecy and objectivity.

Defining Services

The first and maybe the most fundamental hurdle is the absence of a single definition of what is a service. Figure 1.1 is based on but one of several definitions of a service. At a general level, the legal framework governing contracting out for services are the Federal Acquisition Regulation and Defense Federal Acquisition Regulation Supplement, for the Department of Defense. The FAR's definition is that service contracts directly engage the time and effort of a contractor whose primary purpose is to perform a task rather than to furnish a thing.[22] The FAR's list of activities for service contracts includes maintenance, overhaul, repair, servicing, rehabilitation, salvage, modernization, or modification of supplies, systems, or equipment; real property maintenance; housekeeping and base services; advisory and assistance services; communications services; operation of government-owned equipment, real property, and systems; transportation and related services; architect-engineering services; and research and development.[23]

Federal agencies, however, have adopted different classifications. DoD uses one that categorizes services into nine different groups (with forty specific portfolios), including knowledge-based services, R&D, logistics management services, electronic and communication services, and various other categories.[24] The Center for Security and International Studies (CSIS), which sponsors a program in defense industrial initiatives and publishes briefs on trends in outsourcing, divides service contracts into five categories that are like DoD's but not identical. The Office of Management and Budget (OMB) identifies contracted services by five spending categories, several of which have multiple subsidiary object classes.[25] In short, there is no single definition of services.

In addition to the lack of a single definition, DoD, in responding to changes in high-technology areas, often modifies the legal framework for contracting-out. On January 23, 2020, DoD issued "DoD Instruction 5000.02: Operation of the Adaptive Acquisition Framework" (AAF). This instruction establishing the AAF was approved by Ellen M. Lord, undersecretary of defense for acquisition and sustainment. This framework is the most recent effort by DoD to try to accelerate the development and fielding of new programs, products, technologies, and services, still within the terms of the FAR structure. Among other innovations, the AAF recognizes that services are different from products and thus should be contracted differently, as demonstrated by separate pathways and different process milestones.[26]

Data Availability

Another impediment is that the data on the amount and different forms of outsourcing are incomplete. The Federal Procurement Data System (FPDS) is the most comprehensive source of information about federal spending on contracts.[27] The FPDS's data, however, are not complete, and the way data is reported makes it difficult to summarize spending on contracts. As indicative of the serious problems with the data, a recent CRS report on the theme of "Department of Defense Contractors and Troop Levels in Afghanistan and Iraq" explicitly discusses the limitations in the data that are available through an update and modification of the FPDS. The report states the following: "Nevertheless, some observers say that despite their shortcomings, the data available through the beta.SAM.gov Data Bank are substantially more comprehensive than what is available on government procurement activities in most other countries in the world."[28] I read this to mean the US data are better than in Angola, for example. I think it is worth noting that in yet another recent CRS report there is explicit reference on the ambiguity of the data.[29] In Chapter 5, on acquisitions in the context of great power competition, I pay particular attention to the use of OTAs. In his exhaustive (762-page) PhD dissertation on the use of OTAs, Crane Lopes states: "FPDS is a publicly available federal government-wide database those federal agencies are required to use to report data on contract actions whose Estimated value is $3,500 or more.... However, the FAR and DFARS do not require other transactions to be reported in FPDS."[30] The many limitations on the data are a huge impediment to any kind of analysis that aspires to be systematic. For example, in her master of business administration thesis, a US Air Force captain contracting officer states in the conclusion: "Initially the data sample consisted of over 5000 firms, but after scrubbing the data for missing fields, incomplete or inaccurate data, the same was reduced to 437."[31]

The combination of these two problems—multiple categorizations and incomplete thus unreliable data—results in bizarre figures such as the 464,500 contract employees in 2017 for the CRS and 561,239 for Cancian for 2015.[32] The anomaly is also obvious when comparing the data at the outset of this chapter in Figure 1.1. This anomaly may be due to the former counting only full-time equivalents, and the latter not, but one simply has no way of knowing. In any case, the flimsiness of what should be "hard data" makes any kind of quantitative analysis problematic at best.

Secrecy and Proprietary Data

Since the research concerns DoD and the intelligence community (IC), much of the material is classified. As I held a high-security clearance for two decades, serving as rapporteur of the Defense Policy Board, where everything was top secret or above, and having researched and written extensively on other countries' ICs, I at least know what I don't know and therefore hopefully have avoided obvious mistakes. And, as contracting involves competitive bidding, most, if not all, of the information is proprietary. The result is that the great variety of trade publications dealing with national security and defense include short snippets on the awarding of this or that contract, but despite my due diligence I have found that it is impossible to get further information due to classification and the proprietary nature of the product.[33] The combination of the issues of secrecy and proprietary, and the fact that, according to Ash Carter, DoD is the largest and most complex organization in the entire world, does not allow me to utilize the concept, and thus the literature, of "accountability." Given the size, combined with two central factors not allowing for credible data, makes it difficult to determine if much of anything is accountable or not.[34]

Shortage of Objective Information and Analysis

The available literature relating in some way to the topic is spotty. The most objective data, and thus my heavy reliance on it, are produced by both the research and auditing arms of the US Congress: the CRS and GAO, respectively. The bibliography illustrates my extensive use of the reports from CRS—most of which are listed by author in addition to two series on short reports—and from the GAO, all of which are listed under the rubric GAO. The research and publications of these two organizations are directly relevant to policy, since it is at the behest of members or staffers of Congress that they are done. Accordingly, they indicate the priority members of Congress and their staff give to the topic of this book. Both the CRS and the GAO, however, as their staff have put it, "work for Congress," which means they cannot be tasked by others. I was, however, aided by Congressman Jimmy Panetta, whose office interceded on my behalf with the CRS and GAO, to obtain comments that are extremely useful. Both are nonpartisan, but while CRS reports cover many of the topics in this book, they do not cover all of them. GAO reports are basically reports on audits; as the title of the organization suggests, they focus on the accountability of some entity receiving the people's money to the elected representatives or those reporting to them.[35] They can concentrate on accountability, as their authority, as the auditing arm of the Congress, is great, and they focus on very specific issues. This book, however, attempts to deal with DoD outsourcing in general, and thus must draw as widely as possible for relevant information. The book's bibliography should validate my efforts to draw on a wide range of sources. Reports from the RAND Corporation, which is a federally funded research and development center employing highly qualified professional researchers, like the CRS and GAO, are credible. Theses and reports from faculty and students in the acquisition curriculum at the Naval Postgraduate School were also often useful.[36] I also drew upon the research and publications of professionals from the American Enterprise Institute, the Center for a New American Security, the Center for Strategic and International Studies, and the IBM Center for the Business of Government.

Aside from these and from the Packard Commission report, reports from most think tanks and periodic blue-ribbon panels, study groups, committees, and the like, may have some kind of "agenda" related to their funding from some entity, most often the industry or DoD.[37] The reader should remember that the industry, in contrast to DoD and the armed services, can lobby and engage in "strategic communication." Consequently, while I have read and at times draw upon documents by all imaginable sources, it is with caution and skepticism that I use them unless I find other, what I believe to be credible, support. They never build on one another; the reader simply never knows what, if anything, is reformed. A most egregious example draws on the excellent Packard Commission report. The problems it highlighted in 1986 regarding rules, risk-averse personnel, and over-regulation are precisely the problems highlighted by critics today, which will be dealt with in Chapter 6.[38] Then too, they are normally formed of those in the industry. One report that got my (negative) attention draws upon the work of an early contributor to the development of organization theory, one of my main fields in graduate school and the conceptual basis for my PhD dissertation, Chester Barnard, author of *The Functions of the Executive*. The 2014 annual report of DoD on acquisitions begins with a foreword quoting Chester Barnard on the importance of incentives. As Barnard wrote: "Inadequate incentives mean dissolution, or changes of organization purpose, or failure to cooperate. Hence, in all sorts of organizations the affording of adequate incentives becomes the most definitely emphasized task in their existence." The first line of the report itself, by the undersecretary of defense, acquisition, technology, and logistics, states: "By human nature, performance is incentive-driven."[39] In 2012 the federal pay cap on contractors' salaries was $763,029.[40] In that year, the federal pay cap for civilian employees of DoD was $167,000. And considering that there are also active-duty military who are contracting officers, their pay, including benefits, is no greater than that of DoD civilians.[41] With the maximum salaries possible for government employees less than one-quarter what a contractor might legally receive, the scale of what is involved begins to become clear. This is not to say that many contractors receive the pay cap, but for that matter contracting officers receive nothing near the federal pay cap. From my experience, most are in the range of 11 to 13 in a General Schedule (GS) of the US Civil Service, which ranges from 1 to 15, and the maximum in 2015 for GS 11 and 13 was $66,688 and $95,048 respectively.[42] This issue, that of incentives, will be dealt with in Chapter 6.

In addition to documents, I drew on interviews conducted with individuals in the Washington, DC, area. Podcasts also proved to be a useful source of information and are cited appropriately.

About the Book

In this book I focus on two major US national security strategies, or what have been termed strategies. The first, the global war on terrorism, defined US defense and security policy since 9/11 until recently, and the second, great power competition, has gradually assumed increasing prominence since approximately 2014. I have selected them because what is contracted-out presumably follows from the global war on terrorism and great power competition. Consequently, three goals were achieved by choosing these two would-be national security strategies. The first is that the analysis forced me to evaluate how strategic, or real, are these presumed strategies. The second forced me to determine why outsourcing was necessary with these would-be strategies. And third, considering all the challenges to analyzing contracting-out as discussed earlier, there is a great deal of material on the global war on terrorism and great power competition by the CRS and GAO, in addition to a myriad of reports by academics, think tanks, DoD, nongovernmental organizations (NGOs), and others. There is, in short, an abundance of material, including the gold standard set by the CRS and GAO, allowing me to believe that I have found enough credible data to utilize the framework described earlier as a useful lens to look at outsourcing. As neither strategy involves all that DoD contracts out, the book is admittedly not comprehensive but I hope it will serve to highlight the importance of looking at contracting-out whereas previous literature has focused only on various subsets of contracting; mainly private security contractors. What is missing are the myriad of other things and services that the DoD and the IC outsource, and that are essential for their continued functioning. Hopefully, the book will serve as a concrete example that the topic of contracting-out is amenable to research, thereby encouraging others to research and publish on this topic.[43]

Chapter Summaries

The next chapter will summarize the history and highlight some of the main components of the legal and policy framework governing contracting out security. Chapters 3 and 4 will use the perspective of national security strategy to look at outsourcing in the implementation of the global war on terrorism with emphasis on operational contract support (OCS), private security contractors (PSCs), and contract services for the IC. The emphasis in these two chapters will be primarily on the implementation of what was contracted out and the measures taken to achieve success. The reader will see that there were serious problems arising from both OCS and PSCs, and the IC, and they have resulted in very different responses. From my research, the role of the US Congress appears to be central to the very different responses. These two chapters, as they focus on the global war on terrorism, are of necessity retrospective, in that OCS in Iraq and Afghanistan are no longer the focus of US national security that they once were.

Continuing to the present day, the global war on terrorism has been replaced by the national security strategy of great power competition. In this sense the chapters in this part of the book are prospective and can be understood mainly in terms of enhancing the ability of the United States to deter aggression. The key element identified in this strategy, for both DoD and the IC, is obtaining new technologies to ensure the US military and IC can supersede the competition primarily posed by China. This is where contracting must support rapid innovation, and there is a focus on technologies that give advantage over peer or near-peer competitors. There is, then, in contrast to the global war on terrorism, less of an emphasis on implementation, although still important, since the technology is mainly destined for the uniformed military, and there is more emphasis on the mechanisms to acquire the technology. Chapter 5 therefore discusses the nature of the strategy and implications for outsourcing arising thereof, and the opportunity costs incurred by an apparent inability to adapt and innovate. Chapter 6 discusses plans and methods for DoD and the IC to obtain these technologies, focusing heavily on OTAs. As in the discussion in the chapters on the global war on terrorism, the role of the US Congress again looms large, but the implementation is problematic due, in my opinion, largely to the issue of incentives for contracting officers.

Chapter 7, the conclusion, highlights what I determine from the research to be the main problems or challenges. The issue of resources—in which contracting officers, while crucial to the whole process of outsourcing, are poorly compensated in contrast to contractors—is a constant. Beyond this one constant, in utilizing the framework described early in this chapter, I find that the oversight provided, or not, by the US Congress and the absence of education, training, and incentives for those responsible for implementation are particularly important in dealing with the problems identified in the global war on terrorism and great power competition. Regarding the latter topic, it will become clear that the industry is far better positioned than DoD employees in terms of knowledge and incentives in contracting. Indeed, the COs are positively disincentivized to utilize the flexible authorities represented by OTAs. This circumstance, in the context of great power competition, will have important implications on how means are linked with ends as explicitly identified by John Lewis Gaddis.

Notes

1. *CRS In Focus*, "Defense Primer: Department of Defense Contractors" (Washington, DC: Congressional Research Service, December 17, 2021), pp. 1, 3. The most recent data for number of employees are from 2017.

2. Heidi M. Peters, "Department of Defense Contractor and Troop Levels in Afghanistan and Iraq, 2007–2020" (Washington, DC: Congressional Research Service, February 22, 2021), p. 8. Since 2017 DoD refuses to provide data on troop levels (p. 3).

3. Anthony F. Cordesman in "The Reasons for the Collapse of Afghan Forces" lists as one reason: "Giving Afghan forces equipment and support structures that made them indefinitely dependent on contractors and secure contractor facilities"; Washington, DC: Center for Strategic and International Studies, August 17, 2021, p. 9. Earlier, in an op-ed in the *New York Times* of August 25, 2021, the Afghan army commander, General Sami Sadat, in explaining the collapse of the Afghan army, highlighted that the departure, in July 2021, of some 17,000 contractors resulted in the loss of logistics and maintenance support.

4. Matthieu Aikins, "Inside the Fall of Kabul," *New York Times Magazine*, December 10, 2021, p. 41.

5. It is also worth noting that early in the Covid-19 pandemic, DoD declared defense contractors "critical infrastructure," and they had to continue working; http://www.defensenews.com/pentagon2020/03/20pentagon-declares-defense-contractors-critical-infrastructure-must-continue-work. Consistent

with Congressional Research Service policy, the terms "outsourcing" and "contracting out" are used interchangeably.

6. Therefore the information on the "DoD Innovation Ecosystem," which includes not only acquisition authorities whereby contracts are awarded, but also five other components of the "ecosystem," while somewhat useful, is misleading. Without a contract, in accord with an acquisition authority, the other five components are irrelevant. See https://aida.mitre.org/dod-innovation-ecosystem.

7. Ash Carter, *Inside the Five-Sided Box: Lessons from a Lifetime of Leadership in the Pentagon* (New York: Dutton, 2019), p. 9.

8. For FAR and DFARS, see https://www.law.cornell.edu/cfr/text/48/chapter-1, and for DFARS Chapter 2 for US Code. For OTAs, originally these were 10 US Code 2371, 2371b, and 2373. In Chapter 6, I will use the original numbers.

9. Carter, *Inside the Five-Sided Box*, p. 22.

10. J. Ronald Fox, *Defense Acquisition Reform, 1960-2009: An Elusive Goal* (Washington, DC: US Army, Center of Military History, 2021); Tim Weiter, "We Are Lost in the Woods on Acquisition Reform," *Defense News*, May 6, 2021.

11. Morgan Dwyer, Brenen Tidwell, and Alec Blivas, "Cycle Times and Cycles of Acquisition Reform" (Washington, DC: Center for Strategic and International Studies, August 2020).

12. For the most recent explanation by the GAO of high-risk programs, see Government Accountability Office, "High-Risk Series: Dedicated Leadership Needed to Address Limited Progress in Most High-Risk Areas" (Washington, DC, March 2021), GAO-21-119SP.

13. John Lewis Gaddis, *On Grand Strategy* (New York: Penguin, 2019), p. 12.

14. The most recent updating of this framework is found in the introduction and conclusion of Thomas C. Bruneau and Aurel Croissant, eds., *Civil-Military Relations: Control and Effectiveness Across Regimes* (Boulder: Lynne Rienner, 2019). The original formulation is in Thomas C. Bruneau and Florina Cristiana Matei, "Towards a New Conceptualization of Democratization and Civil-Military Relations," *Democratization* 15, no. 5 (December 2008): 909–929.

15. These research and analysis arms are the Congressional Research Service and Government Accountability Office, respectively. Lest one doubt the authority and mechanisms of the Congress to conduct oversight, see the 122-page description and analysis by Christopher M. Davis et al., "Congressional Oversight Manual" (Washington, DC: Congressional Research Service, March 31, 2021).

16. Neither term—"global war on terrorism" nor "great power competition"—makes much sense, but both have been used by DoD and observers,

and will be used in this book mainly for consistency. It is also relevant that there is a CRS series, which is periodically updated, with the title "Renewed Great Power Competition." This publication, the most recent of which I have was updated on February 10, 2022, has an excellent bibliography on all imaginable aspects of great power competition. For useful insights into this "competition," see Michael J. Mazarr, "Understanding Competition: Great Power Rivalry in a Changing International Order—Concepts and Theories" (Santa Monica: RAND, March 2022).

17. See Heidi M. Peters, "Department of Defense Use of Other Transaction Authority: Background, Analysis, and Issues for Congress" (Washington, DC: Congressional Research Service, February 22, 2019), pp. 19–20, for suggestions on possible mechanisms.

18. *CRS In Focus*, "Defense Primer: Department of Defense Contractors" (Washington, DC: Congressional Research Service, December 17, 2021), pp. 1, 3.

19. Ibid., p. 3.

20. See https://www.governing.com/archive/military-civilian-active-duty-employee-workforce-numbers-by-state.html.

21. Robert M. Gates, *Duty: Memoirs of a Secretary at War* (New York: Knopf, 2014), p. 123.

22. Federal Acquisition Regulation 37.101.

23. FAR 37.101(1)-(9). Architect-engineering services, transportation and related services, and research and development services all receive separate treatment under the FAR's regulatory scheme.

24. US Department of Defense (Shay Assad), "Memorandum: Taxonomy for the Acquisition of Services and Supplies & Equipment" (Washington, DC: Office of the Undersecretary of Defense for Acquisition, Technology, and Logistics, August 27, 2012).

25. US Presidency, "Preparation, Submission, and Execution of the Budget" (Washington, DC: White House, July 2020), https://www.whitehouse.gov/wp-content/uploads/2018/06/a11_web_toc.pdf.

26. See the AAF at https://www.esd.whs.mil/Portals/54/Documents/DD/issuances/dodi/500002p.pdf?ver=2019-05-01-151755-110, p. 14.

27. See "Federal Procurement Data System: Next Generation," http://go.usa.gov/3cAtG. FPDS data are available at www.USASpending.gov. For the background of the FPDS and discussion of data accuracy issues, see John F. Sargent Jr. et al., "Defense Acquisitions: How and Where DOD Spends Its Contracting Dollars" (Washington, DC: Congressional Research Service, July 2, 2018).

28. Heidi M. Peters, "Department of Defense Contractor and Troop Levels in Afghanistan and Iraq, 2007–2020" (Washington, DC: Congressional Research Service, February 22, 2021), p. 20.

29. *CRS In Focus,* "Defense Primer: Department of Defense Contractors" (Washington, DC: Congressional Research Service, December 17, 2021), p. 2.

30. Crane Lopes, "Historical Institutionalism and Defense Public Procurement: The Case of Other Transactions Agreements," dissertation, September 19, 2018, pp. 24–25. The 762-page dissertation and much pro-OTA information are available at https://www.strategicinstitute.org. In a communication with me on September 10, 2020, Lopes reported that the data on OTAs are now supposed to be reported in the FPDS, but there is no mechanism to ensure that they are.

31. Alison D. Almonte, "Analysis of Nontraditional Contractors as a Proxy for Innovation Through DOD Other Transaction Agreements," December 2019, p. 41. I do not provide links for material that can easily be found online via Google. I do, however, provide links for material that is less easily obtained, and for podcasts.

32. *CRS In Focus,* "Defense Primer: Department of Defense Contractors," p. 3; Mark F. Cancian, "U.S. Military Forces in 2020" (Washington, DC: CSIS, October 2019), p. 19.

33. I regularly read *Breaking Defense, Defense Daily, Defense News, Defense One,* and *C4ISRNET.* My inquiries to journalists publishing in them for further information on acquisition authorities have not resulted in any useful information.

34. Carter, *Inside the Five-Sided Box,* p. 3. For an excellent discussion of the concept, see Mark Bovens, "Analysing and Assessing Public Accountability: A Conceptual Frameworks" European Governance Paper, (EUROGOV) no. C-06-01, 2006, http://www.connex-network.org/eurogov/pdf/egp-connex-C-06-01.pdf.

35. I include the special inspector general for Iraq reconstruction (SIGIR) and the special inspector general for Afghan reconstruction (SIGAR) along the same lines as the GAO, as their purposes, and staff, are a direct offshoot of the GAO.

36. Much of this research can be found at http://www.acquisitionsresearch.org.

37. US Presidency, "A Quest for Excellence: Report of the U.S. President's Blue Ribbon Commission on Defense Management" (Washington, DC: Packard Commission, June 1986).

38. US Presidency, "A Quest for Excellence: Report of the U.S. President's Blue Ribbon Commission on Defense Management" (Washington, DC: Packard Commission, June 1986), pp. 41–42.

39. US Department of Defense, "Performance of the Defense Acquisition System: 2014 Annual Report" (Washington, DC, June 13, 2014), p. 4, https://www.acq.osd.mil/fo/docs/Performance-of-Defense-Acquisition-System-2014.pdf. The issue of negative, or perverse, incentives is identified

in GAO, "Defense Acquisition: Addressing Incentives Is Key to Further Reform Efforts," testimony before the Senate Committee on Armed Services, April 30, 2014.

40. GAO, "Report to Congressional Committees: Defense Contractors—Information on the Impact of Reducing the Cap on Employee Compensation Costs" (Washington, DC, June 2013), p. 2. The federal pay cap for contractors was reduced to $555,000 for 2020. This was established by Section 702 of the Bipartisan Budget Act of 2013 (Public Law 113-67, December 26, 2013). The act charges the Office of Federal Procurement Policy with annually adjusting the pay cap for contractors.

41. For these data, see *CRS In Focus*, "Regular Military Compensation" (Washington, DC, December 26, 2019). Table 1 shows that a major, or navy lieutenant commander, receives a total of $130,500 including salary, housing, and the like.

42. The federal pay cap for 2021 was $172,500. It seems to me that this relatively low sum is consistent with the philosophy behind A-76, discussed in Chapter 1. That is, the private sector is considered the "engine of growth" in the United States, and government employment is considered almost parasitic, feeding off the private sector.

43. Two obvious topics for research are the contracting-out of military housing and the military healthcare system. Both receive extensive coverage in the media.

2

The Historical and Legal Context

MY PURPOSE IN THIS CHAPTER IS TO PROVIDE INFORMATION ABOUT three incontrovertible facts; without this information, the rest of the book will not make much sense. The first is that DoD leads all US federal agencies in contracting-out.[1] Second, according to the Government Accountability Office, DoD contract management is high risk,[2] which means, in line with the title of GAO "Accountability," DoD contract management is not fully accountable. And third, despite a spate of "acquisition reform efforts" over decades, the Federal Acquisition Regulation remains the primary legal and policy basis for contracting-out. I believe the succinct practical guidance that follows emphatically makes this point: "If you plan to contract with the federal government, the Federal Acquisition Regulation (FAR) will serve as your 'bible.' . . . Currently, the FAR includes more than 1,600 pages and is divided into 53 parts, each dealing with a separate aspect of the procurement process."[3]

For this long history I draw heavily on the brief version provided in the Center for a New American Security's (CNAS) *Contracting in Conflicts: The Path to Reform*, and online sources.[4]

The Early Years: Revolutionary War to Civil War

During the birth of the United States during the Revolutionary War, private Americans and private businesses supported the war effort.

Indeed, due to the very nature of a war of independence, there was no national army nor were there other national institutions to begin with. Private support to the army fighting for independence from Great Britain took the form of "engineering, food, transportation, medical and carpentry services."[5] All of this was at the request of both the Continental Congress and General George Washington, as the nucleus that would eventually become the US government experienced shortages of every type and variety. At that time and in that context, contracting was often the only way to prosecute the war. There was a lack of institutions to provide oversight in the middle of the war for independence, and in chaotic conditions, corruption and inefficiency were prevalent. To begin to remedy this situation, in 1781 Congress made Superintendent of Finance Robert Morris responsible for supplying the war effort. To this end, private services were essential to helping Morris accomplish this task, which included supplying the army, labor support to the war effort, and cooking services.[6] It is worth noting that the Americans did not have a monopoly on the use of contractors. King George III of Great Britain used state-sponsored contractors in the form of not only Hessians, but also troops contracted from other Germanic entities to fight in the colonies against the Americans. With victory and independence, presidents, Congress, and government officials sought to address the deficiencies apparent in the war effort by attempting to centralize procurement and promote oversight, by adopting rules for low-bid contracts, and by focusing on the quality and timeliness of products and services.

Despite improvements in the process and servicing of American military forces after the Revolutionary War, reliance on private contracting continued to be characterized by uneven progress, corruption, and generally much room for improvement. Further action to gain more control involved legislation passed to lay the foundation of military procurement, including a competitive bid process, prohibitions on members of Congress profiteering from service contracts, and division of acquisitions responsibility among different agencies to prevent abuse.[7] Nevertheless, US military forces continued to experience hardship and limits in operational effectiveness in the reliance on contractors. According to Deborah Kidwell, a notable improvement appeared during this time period with the Mexican American War (1846–1848), which saw the nation, its armed forces, and supporting contractor services field, supply, and effectively support forces away from the country's center of gravity on the Eastern Seaboard. According to Kidwell, the resulting victory for the United States illustrated how far the armed forces and contractor support services had progressed. The Mexican American War is widely recognized as the start of increasing standardization and professionalization, which combined with $78 million worth of contracted goods and services to "supply expeditionary armies better than ever before in the nation's history."[8]

Despite the success in supporting the war effort in the Mexican American War, the institutions, contractors, and armed forces of Americans on both sides of the Civil War (1861–1865) proved to be less than effective in the maelstrom of internecine conflict. As both the Union and the Confederacy fielded armies and fought battles with hundreds of thousands of men, the industry, services, and general mobilization to support such armies rapidly outstripped the capacity of existing governmental institutions. The tremendous requirements and wartime conditions provided ample opportunity for war-profiteering and fraud, while established government practice of selecting low-bid contracts resulted often in inferior products being provided by contractors.[9] For the Union, hence the US government, the degree of fraud in contracting for the war effort resulted in the passage of the False Claims Act in 1863. The False Claims Act provided the basis for the government to go after contractors who knowingly committed fraud on contracts and included provision for whistleblowers or "relators" to bring instances of fraud to light for proper investigation.[10] In an early instance of contracting out intelligence functions, Union armies under General George McClellan enlisted the Allan Pinkerton detective agency to provide intelligence-collection capacity.[11] In the Civil War the private sector was heavily mobilized to support the war effort, which was essential for both sides. Union victory, in which no small part can be credited to its advantage in industry and general capacity of contracted services, still came at the cost of immense loss of life.

World War I to World War II

Whereas the Mexican American War started the US military's venture in expeditionary warfare and the requisite support of forces away from the country's center, the Civil War necessitated an internal turn as war came to the US heartland. Following the Civil War, the United States once again took up an outward focus that, although varying over the years with many internal forces advocating for a continued insular vision, culminated in US involvement as an Associated power in World War I and as an Allied power in World War II. This involvement of US armed forces on a truly global scale saw the total mobilization of the US private sector and contractor services to support the war effort, which was similar to private sector support in the Civil War but focused outwardly and of a different magnitude of scale. This period saw an enlargement of US international obligations and the beginnings of its superpower status.

While the Civil War already saw the importance of industry and the private sector in supporting the armed forces, World War I further demonstrated this trend as war capacity became increasingly synonymous with industrial capacity. The scale of the war again required the use of contractors and increasingly necessitated integration among institutions, citizens, and private sector. Indeed, the War Industries Board, "populated by business and government leaders, harnessed American industrial might to its war machine through production management, coordinated purchases, and assured that needed resources reached the battlefield."[12] Throughout World War I, as the volume of products and services provided by government contractors increased, so too did the need for more oversight. Congress worked to address the need for increased oversight by focusing on the contracting process itself. Reforms to the contracting process included mandating the competitive bid process, banning advance payments, and introducing limits to manufacturer profits.[13] As the country mobilized on the home front for World War I, the need to support the American Expeditionary Forces (AEF) fighting on the Western Front grew and war expenditure proved to be overwhelming. Beyond the obvious need to transport and supply an army across the Atlantic, specific services required included construction of railroads and postal services, all done by over 85,000 contractors.[14]

In the aftermath of World War I and as the technology of warfare became more sophisticated with the introduction and refinement of the airplane, the tank, and generally increased mechanization, contractor services and the importance of contractors continued to grow in importance in making up for gaps in government knowledge and capacity. The pace of technological development and increased sophistication continued during the interwar years of the 1920s and 1930s to the extent that more oversight on contractor work became routine practice. For example, on the issue of airplane procurement, "quality checks of materials and workmanship were performed from design to final acceptance of the product."[15]

Prior to the official entry of the United States into World War II as an Allied power in the aftermath of the Japanese attack on Pearl Harbor, and even as US military mobilization had already started, the highlight of initial efforts of the private sector and contracting was contributing to US government programs supporting friendly powers such as Great Britain, France, the Soviet Union, and China against Germany, Japan, and Italy. These programs included the much-celebrated Lend-Lease Act, under which military equipment and aid produced by US contractors were provided to the Allied combatants. In North Africa and the Middle East, contractors were provided by the United States to help the Allies with maintenance and other support services.[16]

As the United States officially entered World War II as an active combatant, contractors were already on the front lines. Indeed, civilian employees of the Morrison-Knudsen Corporation were supporting the Marine garrison of Wake Island when the Japanese attacked the island in December 1941.[17] Contracted to perform base infrastructure construction, these civilian contractors were caught in the middle of an invasion and were captured when the island surrendered to the Japanese. The involvement of contractors closer to the front lines continued throughout World War II as the plans of the United States and Allied nations to build the infrastructure and forward support facilities for the men and equipment fighting a multifront war depended on contractor involvement and labor. This integration of effort saw about 730,000 contractors supporting 5.4 million US military personnel.[18]

This integration, as reflected by the experience of civilian contractors on Wake Island, saw increased dangers for civilian contractors, as enemy forces could kill or capture contractors supporting frontline troops. While contractors did not supplant frontline troops and instances of contractors being armed were extremely limited, the proximity to combat was undeniable given that even civilian population centers experienced the effects of war, given strategic bombing and targeting of centers of production by all sides.

Despite the increased presence of contractors closer to the front lines, this was overshadowed by the themes of increased centralization of government contracting and general mobilization of the private sector with suitable amendments to contracting during wartime. Despite the passage of the Lend-Lease Act and the role of the act in kick-starting the US war economy, the War Production Board was created by President Franklin D. Roosevelt in Executive Order 9024 in 1942 to further meet the requirements of production and the need for centralized direction. The War Production Board had multiple tasks that included "general direction over the war procurement and production program" and government involvement in "war procurement and production, including purchasing, contracting, specifications."[19] Whereas at that time normal government contracting practice was to rely on the competitive bid process for purchasing and contracts, there was already discussion on limiting profits of contractors even during the lead-up to the entrance of the United States into World War II. Prewar, contractors for naval vessels and naval aircraft were subject to varying profit limiting provisions, including profit limits of 8 percent, 10 percent, or 12 percent depending on the specific time period, until the passage of the Second Revenue Act of 1940 (October 8), which removed profit-limiting provisions.[20] As peacetime practice clashed with wartime requirements, War Production Board chairman Donald Nelson issued an order removing competitive bidding as the standard means of government contracting practice.[21] Given the requirements of mobilization and fighting a global war, the World War II experience demonstrated that the US government was willing and able to modify or in many cases completely abrogate preexisting contracting practice to meet changing requirements.

Cold War to Present Day

At the conclusion of World War II, the War Production Board dissolved, and the wartime measures gave way as the sense of national urgency subsided. In this backdrop of the immediate aftermath of World War II and the early Cold War, contracting in support of national security and DoD returned to peacetime practice with the removal of profit-limiting schemes and the return of the competitive bid process, together with varying degrees of negotiated contracts, as acceptable means in government contracting. Some wartime themes remained, including more centralization of the government contracting and embodied by the National Security Act of 1947 and the Armed Services Procurement Act of 1947. These two acts laid the basis for centralization and standardization of defense contracting and "standardized purchasing methods for all the military departments."[22] The Armed Services Procurement Act led to the Armed Services Procurement Regulation and had as its goal the "consolidation of the diverse service-specific rules and regulations that had governed military procurement since the Civil War,"[23] and required advertisement of contract opportunities. In recognition of the success of the wartime War Production Board and with a view toward potential conflict and mobilization resulting from increased tensions of the Cold War and the outbreak of the Korean War, the Defense Production Act of 1950 codified extraordinary powers to the government for defense and war mobilization. The Defense Production Act helped set conditions for working links between the government and the private sector and played a role in "forming the basis of modern defense acquisition—the management of industrial capabilities, human capital, financial resources, and science and technology to provide the means of modern war."[24]

The role of the private sector and government contracting for defense and national security continued to grow during the Cold War with a shift of focus and resources increasingly toward the private sector. The result of this shift is visible with the reduction of government-owned war plants and heavy to almost complete reliance on private shipyards for naval construction and repair.[25] In many ways, the role and expansion of private sector capacity during

World War II resulting from wartime requirements carried over into the Cold War as the Cold War continued to see an elevated demand for procurement, much of which was fulfilled by government contract with the private sector. The 1960 Armed Services Procurement Regulation highlighted the need for greater government control over the contracting process, and under Secretary of Defense Robert McNamara the Department of Defense established the Defense Contract Administration Services, which evolved into the Defense Contract Management Command and eventually the Defense Contract Management Agency, to provide centralized contracts administration service and oversight on contractor performance.[26]

While the shift toward greater reliance on private sector contractors resulted in cost overruns for many defense contracts, other factors such as "inflation, Vietnam, and commercial competition for skilled labor and resources" also need to be accounted for.[27] It is interesting to note that the very competition that is often held to be an advantage in the private sector in terms of spurring innovation and efficiency may have negative results for defense contracting as contractors seek to fulfill both commercial and defense contracts using limited means of production. Perhaps an even bigger factor contributing to the theme of cost overrun was the "unanticipated unknowns" resulting from technological progress and the parallel, predictable inability of contractors to make accurate cost estimates.[28] The initiatives that attempted to address these cost overruns, often referred to as the McNamara Reforms, proved to be ineffective.

As the Cold War continued past Vietnam and into the Reagan era, the defense expansion that occurred again changed the conditions for contracting in support of defense and national security.

The Meaning of Contracting-Out and the A-76 Process

A 2008 CRS report gives a sense of what is involved in, and the extensive legal basis for, government privatization, which will be the focus for the remainder of this chapter.

Sometimes called contracting out, "outsourcing" refers to an agency engaging a private firm to perform an agency function or provide a service.... Federal outsourcing policy is governed by the FAR and the Federal Activities Inventory Reform (FAIR) Act of 1998 (Public Law 105-270). FAIR requires agencies to produce inventories of "commercial activities"—those that are not "inherently governmental" and able to be acquired from the private sector—that may be put up for competitive sourcing. OMB's Circular A-76 provides agencies with specific directions for undertaking competitive sourcing.[29]

The US government has formalized the process involved in making these decisions in the A-76 competition.[30] The exceptions are what are defined as "inherently governmental functions," which cannot be contracted out.[31]

Circular A-76 was most recently revised on May 29, 2003, during the administration of President Barack Obama. In contrast to his predecessor, President George W. Bush, Obama is not thought of as a pro-privatization president. Even so, his administration's text is as follows: "In the process of governing, the Government should not compete with its citizens. The competitive enterprise system, characterized by individual freedom and initiative, is the primary source of national economic strength. In recognition of this principle, it has been and continues to be the general policy of the Government to rely on commercial sources to supply the products and services the Government needs."[32] In other words, rather than assuming that the government, including in national security, has a monopoly, the legal basis in the United States codified in Circular A-76 is precisely the opposite. During a certain period, which is discussed in the aforementioned report, DoD engaged in competitions to determine if a certain process or institution within the domain of DoD should be privatized.

It should be no surprise that the process, or legal basis, for contracting-out, for providing "the people's money" to for-profit firms, "the industry," is extremely elaborate. I believe the statement with which I began this chapter captures this well: "If you plan to contract with the federal government, the Federal Acquisition Regulation (FAR) will serve as your 'bible.'"[33] Rather than going into grueling detail on the FAR, I think it most efficient to draw the reader's attention to an excellent summary of the main points of the FAR.[34] While there have been "acquisition reforms" since the FAR took effect in 1984, from all that I can gather, all of them—including the most recent "Operation of the Adaptive Acquisition Framework" emanating from DoD Instruction 5000.02 of January 23, 2020—are still within the limits of the FAR. On this very topic I received an email message from the main expert on the issue of acquisitions at the Congressional Research Service. She wrote: "DOD tends to throw around the word 'innovation' frequently, and not always in reference to a genuinely innovative capability. Sometimes, 'innovation' to DOD is nothing more than rearranging the deck chairs."[35]

The FAR Forever?

In conducting research for this book, I have spent a great deal of time attempting to determine if any of the so-called innovations in the legal basis for awarding contracts, for contracting-out, replace the FAR. Until now nobody has written or said anything to make me believe the FAR has been superseded. That is, until the creation and adoption of the OTA, which will be described and analyzed in Chapter 6. It must be stated here, and up front, that Ash Carter, as secretary of defense, took the lead in adopting this alternative contracting mechanism. In a section of his book titled *Building Bridges to Silicon Valley*, he discusses creation of the Defense Innovation Unit, which, as we will see in Chapter 6, works mainly, if not exclusively, with OTAs.[36]

Conclusion

This chapter should make it clear that contracting-out by the US government to private firms has a long history. Unlike in most other countries, the government is discouraged from doing something that the private sector can do. The most recent and specific legal basis for this process is stipulated in Circular A-76.

Notes

1. "In FY 2017, DOD obligated more money on federal contracts ($320 billion in current dollars) than all other governmental agencies combined."

Moshe Schwartz, John F. Sargent Jr., and Christopher T. Mann, "Defense Acquisitions: How and Where DOD Spends Its Contracting Dollars" (Washington, DC: Congressional Research Service, July 2, 2018), Summary.

2. "Over the years since we added this area to our High-Risk List, we have made numerous recommendations related to this high-risk issue, 18 of which were made since the last high-risk update in February 2017. As of November 2018, 41 recommendations related to this high-risk area are open"; https://www.gao.gov/mobile/high-risk/dod_contract_management/why_did-study. See also GAO, "High-Risk Series: Substantial Efforts Needed to Achieve Greater Progress on High-Risk Areas" (Washington, DC: Government Accountability Office, March 2019).

3. Scott A. Stanberry, *Federal Contracting Made Easy*, 4th ed. (Tysons Corner, VA: Management Concepts, 2013), p. 25. Lest the reader think that a "how to" book is not credible, he or she might want to consult the 612 page double-pane John T. Jones Jr., *Government Contract Law: The Deskbook for Procurement Professionals*, 4th ed. (Chicago: American Bar Association, 2017).

4. Richard Fontaine and John Nagl, "Contracting in Conflicts: The Path to Reform" (Washington, DC: Center for a New American Security, June 2010). For much more detailed histories, see, for example, James F. Nagle, *A History of Government Contracting*, 2d ed. (Washington, DC: George Washington University Press, 2005); Erna Risch, *Quartermaster Support of the Army, A History of the Corps 1775–1939* (Washington, DC: US Army Center of Military History, 1989).

5. Fontaine and Nagl, "Contracting in Conflicts," p. 8.

6. Deborah Kidwell, *Private War, Public Fight? The United States and Private Military Companies* (Lulu.com, 2011), p. 10.

7. Ibid., p. 11.

8. Ibid., p. 12.

9. Ibid.

10. *The False Claims Act: A Primer*, https://www.justice.gov/sites/default/files/civil/legacy/2011/04/22/C-FRAUDS_FCA_Primer.pdf, p. 2.

11. Fontaine and Nagl, "Contracting in Conflicts," p. 8.

12. Kidwell, *Private War, Public Fight?* p. 13.

13. Ibid.

14. Fontaine and Nagl, "Contracting in Conflicts," p. 8.

15. Janet McDonnell, "A History of Defense Contract Administration," March 5, 2020, https://www.dcma.mil/News/Article-View/Article/2100501/a-history-of-defense-contract-administration.

16. Kidwell, *Private War, Public Fight?* p. 13.

17. Ibid., p. 1.

18. Fontaine and Nagl, "Contracting in Conflicts," p. 10.

19. "Executive Order 9024 Establishing the War Production Board" (Washington, DC: American Presidency Project, January 16, 1942), https://

www.presidency.ucsb.edu/documents/executive-order-9024-establishing-the-war-production-board.

20. B. W. Patch, "War Contracts and Profit Limitation," Editorial Research Report 1942 (vol. 11), https://library.cqpress.com/cqresearcher/document.php?id=cqresrre1942110600.

21. Ibid.

22. Janet McDonnell, "A History of Defense Contract Administration," March 5, 2020, https://www.dcma.mil/News/Article-View/Article/2100501/a-history-of-defense-contract-administration.

23. Shannon Brown, *Providing the Means of War: Historical Perspectives on Defense Acquisition, 1945–2000* (Washington, DC: US Army Center of Military History and Industrial College of the Armed Forces, 2005), p. 9, https://history.army.mil/html/books/070/70-87-1/CMH_Pub_70-87-1.pdf.

24. Ibid., p. 10.

25. Ibid., p. 40.

26. McDonnell, "A History of Defense Contract Administration."

27. Brown, *Providing the Means of War*, p. 83.

28. Ibid., p. 84.

29. Kevin Kosar, "Privatization and the Federal Government: An Introduction" (Washington, DC: Congressional Research Service, December 28, 2006), p. 15.

30. For the latest information on the A-76 process, see Heidi M. Peters, "A-76 Competitions in the Department of Defense" (Washington, DC: Congressional Research Service, June 2, 2020). This 2020 report follows two, much longer, CRS reports of 2003 and 2005. An update on A-76 will be provided in Chapter 3.

31. Inherently governmental functions will be dealt with in Chapter 3.

32. See "OMB Circular A-76," https://obamawhitehouse.archives.gov/omb/circulars_a076 (hereinafter).

33. Stanberry, *Federal Contracting Made Easy*, p. 25.

34. See Kate M. Manuel et al., "The Federal Acquisition Regulation (FAR): Answers to Frequently Asked Questions" (Washington, DC: Congressional Research Service, February 3, 2015).

35. Email from CRS expert on November 6, 2020. Staff of Congress, including the CRS, must remain anonymous.

36. Ash Carter, *Inside the Five-Sided Box* (New York: Dutton, 2019), pp. 326–331.

3

Supporting the Global War on Terrorism

WHILE THE US EXPERIENCES ABROAD IN THE GLOBAL WAR ON TERRORism, which included invading and occupying Afghanistan and Iraq in 2001 and 2003, respectively, are not generally considered strategic successes, the explanation does not lie with the extensive use of contractors. On the other hand, neither did extensive use of contractors guarantee success. Further, as stated in the first line of the executive summary of the final report of Commission on Wartime Contracting in Iraq and Afghanistan in August 2011: "At least $31 billion, and possibly as much as $60 billion, has been lost to contract waste and fraud in America's contingency operations in Iraq and Afghanistan."[1] One can only imagine how much more was lost in the intervening ten years. The fundamental reason for the two failures was the lack of a strategy that included both the use of contractors and the perils of "nation building" in these two extremely underdeveloped countries.

Themes of Continuing Relevance Regarding Contracting-Out

I have found that several themes I became familiar with in earlier research, in 2008 and 2009, continue to have relevance today, and may well continue to have relevance in the future. Three of these merit discussion here, for they raise the issue of the political processes involved in DoD outsourcing. While interviewing members of the industry during seven research trips in the Washington, DC, area, virtually all of them were extremely critical of the work of the Commission on Wartime Contracting in Iraq and Afghanistan, which had been created by Congress in 2008, and which issued interim reports in June 2009 and February 2011, and a final report in August 2011. I interviewed staff members and one commissioner, and I was impressed with the scope, competence, and seriousness of the commission's work.[2] I was amazed to see, therefore, by August 1, 2012, a year later, that DoD had taken or planned action on only about half of the recommendations, and Department of State and the US Agency for International Development (USAID) about one-third.[3] What was even more amazing is that between 2012 and the release of the National Defense Authorization Act (NDAA) for fiscal year 2020, there was little or no action on the commission's recommendations. However, the NDAA for fiscal year 2020, in Section 887, mandated that the GAO would do two reports—one on contingency contracting in general and another on private security contractors. Both of these GAO reports are now available and are extremely critical of DoD; the former reads, in the first sentence under "What GAO Found": "The Department of Defense (DOD) has taken steps to implement 16 of 30 recommendations it agreed to address and that were made by the Commission on Wartime Contracting in Iraq and Afghanistan."[4] As there were numerous critical reports on contingency contracting by the CRS, GAO, DoD inspector general, and others, in the intervening eight years, one must wonder why the recommendations were never implemented.[5] I personally have no insight into the politics involved during both Democratic and Republican administrations.

However, I do have insights on the politics involved in the definition of inherently governmental functions.[6] An inherently governmental function is one that must be performed by a governmental employee and cannot be performed by a contractor. As there were multiple definitions of the concept, several members of Congress wanted one definition of inherently governmental functions and tasked the Office of Management and Budget to come up with one through a process of inputs. Ultimately, the political process resulted in not one but two definitions of inherently governmental functions.[7] The theme of inherently governmental function will be dealt with as well later in this chapter.

The A-76 process, which epitomizes the pro–free enterprise system dominant in the United States, was "suspended" in the fiscal year 2010 NDAA, and despite the stipulated reforms that were implemented by DoD, the moratorium continues today.[8] It is fairly clear that it was the efforts of the public services unions that led to the suspension. Whereas CRS reports are strictly nonpartisan and GAO reports are heavily saccharine, any issue involving the sums of money that go into outsourcing undoubtedly has a political dimension. I would hope that future research on these topics will include the political dimension best learned through personal interviews, but given the restrictions resulting from Covid-19, I was unable to do so in this book.

Contingency Contracting

According to a GAO summary of the relevant legislation and DoD policy on the topic of this chapter, the following definition is offered:

> Contingency contracting is the process of obtaining goods, services, and construction in support of contingency operations, and DOD identifies this contracting as a part of Operational Contract Support (OCS). Contingency contracting entails the use of contractor personnel from as many as 195 countries who comprise a critical component of the department's ability to provide forces and support U.S. military capabilities.[9]

Table 3.1 indicates the reliance on contractors in Iraq.[10] While the data in the table are from 2008, more recent data show an increased reliance on contractors vis-à-vis US uniformed forces. According to a CRS report, drawing upon US Central Command (CENTCOM) quarterly census reports, in the fourth quarter of fiscal year 2017 there were 11,100 US armed forces personnel in Afghanistan, and 23,659 contractors, and more recent data, from the fourth quarter of fiscal year 2020 showed 22,562 contractors. The same data for the same quarter in Iraq and Syria showed "up to 5,262 U.S. armed forces and 4,609 contractors, and in quarter 4 of 2020 4,826 contractors."[11]

In terms of "the people's money," a recent GAO report states the following: "DOD obligations for contracts in support of contingency

Table 3.1 Presence of Contractor Personnel During US Military Operations

Conflict	Estimated Personnel (thousands) Contractor[a]	Military	Estimated Ratio of Contractor to Military Personnel[a]
Revolutionary War	2	9	1 to 6
War of 1812	n/a	38	n/a
Mexican-American War	6	33	1 to 6
Civil War	200	1,000	1 to 5
Spanish-American War	n/a	35	n/a
World War I	85	2,000	1 to 24
World War II	734	5,400	1 to 24
Korea	156	393	1 to 2.5
Vietnam	70	359	1 to 5
Gulf War	9	500	1 to 55[b]
Balkans	20	20	1 to 1
Iraq Theater as of Early 2008[c]	190	200	1 to 1

Sources: Congressional Budget Office based on data from William W. Epley, "Civilian Support of Field Armies," *Army Logistician* 22 (November–December 1990): 30–35; Steven J. Zamparelli, "Contractors on the Battlefield: "What Have We Signed up For?" *Air Force Journal of Logistics* 23, no. 3 (Fall 1999): 10–19; US Department of Defense, *Report on DoD Program for Planning, Managing, and Accounting for Contractor Services and Contractor Personnel During Contingency Operations* (Washington, DC: October 2017), p. 12.

Notes: n/a = not available.

a. For some conflicts, the estimated number of contractor personnel includes civilians employed by the US government. However, because most civilians present during military operations are contractor personnel, the inclusion of government civilians should not significantly affect the calculation of contractor personnel to military personnel.

b. The government of Saudi Arabia provided significant amounts of products and services during Operations Desert Shield and Desert Storm. Personnel associated with these provisions are not included in the data or the ratio.

c. For this study, the Congressional Budget Office considers the following countries to be part of the Iraqi Theater: Iraq, Bahrain, Jordan, Kuwait, Oman, Qatar, Saudi Arabia, Turkey, and the United Arab Emirates.

operations totaled about $158 billion from calendar year 2009 to 2019. According to DOD reports, contractor personnel continued in 2019 to outnumber deployed service members in military operations in Iraq and Afghanistan."[12]

Roles of Contractors in Contingency Operations

In view of the number of contractors, the amount of money spent, and the variety of their roles, I feel I should provide some information on a topic not noted in the preceding paragraphs—that is, their roles. The most useful approach I have found detailing the extent to which DoD has come to rely on contractors is that proposed by Peter Singer, of the Brookings Institution, an early and reasonably objective analyst of contingency contracting.[13]

Singer's typology categorizes contingency contractors according to the services they provide, based on their proximity to the front line and relationship of their contract performance to actual hostilities.[14] As illustrated in Figure 3.1, military provider firms are defined by their focus on the tactical environment at the forefront of the battlespace. These firms typically fill military specialties on the battlefield, and in some cases may engage in actual fighting. A typical example is DynCorp International, and the most (in)famous is Blackwater USA. Military consulting firms provide advisory and training services. For Singer, these firms provide strategic, operational, and organizational analysis, but do not operate on the battlefield itself. They are more like a private business consulting firm. Singer's third grouping is military support firms, which provide supplementary military services. Included in this category are firms providing nonlethal aid and assistance, including logistics, intelligence, technical support, supply, and transportation.[15] Generally, these contractors are farther physically from the conduct of hostilities.

While I believe Singer's typology is useful in capturing the main dimensions of contingency contractors' functions, it has limitations.[16]

In fact, the services that DoD outsources in contingency operations are incredibly varied, requiring great simplification for any model. A synopsis of this variety is found in a Government Accountability Office report:

Figure 3.1 Battlefield Frontline

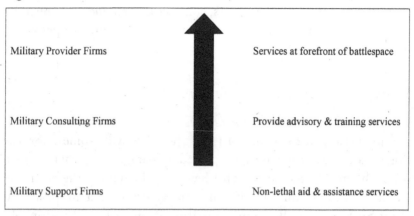

Source: Peter Singer's "Tip of the Spear" typology of service contractor supporting overseas contingency operations.

Contractors located throughout the Middle East and Southwest Asia provide U.S. forces with such services as linguistic support, equipment maintenance, base operations support, and security support. In Iraq and Afghanistan, contractors provide deployed U.S. forces with communication services; interpreters who accompany military patrols; base operations support (e.g., food and housing); weapons systems maintenance; intelligence analysis; and a variety of other types of support. Contractors provide logistics support that includes parts and equipment distribution, ammunition accountability and control, port support activities, and support to weapons systems and tactical vehicles.[17]

In order to give a sense of the extent of outsourcing in contingency operations in Iraq and Afghanistan, I will provide some information on two programs, one at the bottom, the Logistics Civil Augmentation Program (LOGCAP), and one at the top of Singer's spear, private security contractors. The latter, PSCs, are included, although relatively small in funds appropriated, due to the outsize (largely negative) attention they have received in the media and academic studies, and as they raise a key issue in contracting out—namely the meaning of inherently governmental functions.

Logistics Civil Augmentation Program

LOGCAP is a US Army program providing logistics and engineering support for contingency base construction and base operational support-related services.[18] Established in 1985, LOGCAP supplies a large variety of goods and services to support contingency operations. If US forces deploy, contractor support is then available to a commander as an option.[19] LOGCAP is basically a single, centrally managed worldwide contingency operation planning and services contract. Through four iterations, LOGCAP has been used to support US forces in operations in Somalia, Haiti, Bosnia, Iraq, Afghanistan, Kuwait, and other countries. LOGCAP's support of US troops in Iraq was the largest ever.[20]

The Army, Air Force, and Navy each currently manage their own separate engineering and logistics contracts to employ civilian contractors during overseas contingency operations. Drawing directly from Karen LeDoux's article, I provide here a paraphrased summary from the contracting firm KBR regarding its LOGCAP III work in support of Operation Iraqi Freedom to give a sense of the scale of work performed under LOGCAP contracts.

In November 2002, KBR deployed to prepare Camp Arifjan in Kuwait for the anticipated influx of US troops. Since that time (until 2005), KBR has:

- Prepared more than 160 million meals.
- Washed more than 6.2 million bundles of laundry.
- Produced more than 1 billion gallons of potable water.
- Transported more than 300 million gallons of fuel.
- Hosted more than 18 million patrons at morale, welfare, and recreation facilities.
- Delivered more than 560,000 bags of mail.
- Logged more than 50 million miles transporting supplies and equipment for the military (with more than 900 trucks on the road each day).

KBR had 48,000 employees and subcontractors deployed to Kuwait and Iraq to support the US military. Although KBR and its subcontractors have lost several of their personnel to hostile actions, they continue to honor their commitment to ensure that the troops serving in Iraq have the best food, shelter, and quality of life possible.[21]

Umbrella military support contracts like LOGCAP are huge. In January 2005 the estimated value of one contract for the Army was $15 billion.[22] The ten-year LOGCAP III contract, awarded to KBR in 2001 for support in Iraq, Afghanistan, Kuwait, and the Republic of Georgia, included services valued at $35.7 billion.[23] In order to address perceived problems with the LOGCAP III contract, in 2008 the Army awarded the LOGCAP IV contract to three companies: KBR, Fluor Intercontinental, and DynCorp International. The LOGCAP IV contracts are indefinite-delivery/indefinite-quantity (IDIQ) contracts with one base year and nine option years. Each contract has a maximum value of $5 billion per year. More recently, in 2019 the Army awarded the LOGCAP V contract to four contractors: Vertus, KBR, Fluor Intercontinental, and a partnership of PAE-Parsons Global Logistics Services.[24] The Army anticipated spending approximately $3–3.5 billion per year on this contract, and total contract value is capped at $82 billion over ten years.[25]

Not surprisingly with such huge contracts, problems arise. For example, the Commission on Wartime Contracting in Iraq and Afghanistan cited the Army for favoring the use of existing task and delivery order contracts like LOGCAP over more competitive and targeted contract vehicles, and calculated that the lack of competition on the LOGCAP III and IV contracts resulted in $3.3 billion in waste.[26] The special inspector general for Afghan reconstruction also has documented instances of human trafficking by LOGCAP contractor employees.[27]

Private Security Contractors

Beginning in Iraq in 2003, the provision of security was outsourced to private firms, most of them with limited experience in providing contracting support of this nature. This was a first for the United States in that, during the Balkan wars (1991–1995), US and other

North Atlantic Treaty Organization (NATO) member troops provided security. It was not an absolute first in that some of the private security contractors had previous experience in Africa and Southeast Asia. In addition to the fact that in both Iraq and Afghanistan the whole countries became battlegrounds, there were two more reasons for outsourcing security. First was a lack of US military personnel to provide security. At the end of the Cold War, the US Army went from 732,000 active-duty personnel in 1990 to 409,000 in 1997; for the three armed services, including the Marines, the numbers were 2,043,705 in 1990, to 1,438,562 in 1997.[28] This factor was exacerbated by the desire of Secretary of Defense Donald Rumsfeld (2001–2006) to demonstrate that the Iraq invasion and pacification could be accomplished with a lean fighting force, and that technology would be a sufficient force multiplier. A success in Iraq would justify his policy promoting defense "transformation" over a traditional buildup of forces. Whereas the United States deployed 500,000 troops in the 1991 war against Iraq, the 2003 invasion kept troop levels to about 150,000. General Eric Shinseki, Army chief of staff, expressed his disagreement with this policy while being questioned before Congress in 2003. Shortly thereafter, Secretary of Defense Rumsfeld announced Shinseki's replacement, some eighteen months before his scheduled retirement.

Second, the US military cannot provide security protection to personnel who are not members of DoD: "The military provides security to contractors and government civilians only if they deploy with the combat force or directly support the military's mission."[29] The Department of State, USAID, and others involved in reconstruction in Iraq and Afghanistan had no option but to contract out to meet their security needs by employing private security contractors. Ignoring the need for reliable protection was not an option. The Department of State's Bureau of Diplomatic Security is not set up to handle ongoing operations in war zones. Such needs were equally true for USAID, as well as for NGOs and private firms. Since a huge element of what turned out to be "nation building," or "reconstruction," in Iraq and Afghanistan was led by the Department of State and USAID, and since the US military could not provide security, there was no option but to contract out for security providers.

The outsourcing of security entailed four very different functions: *static security*, to protect fixed or static sites such as housing areas, reconstruction work sites, or government buildings; *convoy security*, to protect convoys traveling in Iraq or Afghanistan; *security escorts*, to protect individuals traveling in unsecured areas in Iraq and Afghanistan; and *personal security details*, to provide protective security to high-ranking individuals.[30] Since in both Iraq and Afghanistan virtually all of the country was considered a conflict zone, the need for security was palpable. It is no wonder, then, that the numbers of private security contractors were very great. The high point in Iraq was the third quarter of fiscal year 2009, when there were 15,279 private security contractors out of a total of 119,706 contractors; and in Afghanistan the high point was the third quarter of fiscal year 2012, when there were 28,686 private security contractors out of a total of 113,736 contractors.[31]

While outsourcing in Iraq and Afghanistan ultimately drew a high level of attention, from the media, the public, and the US Congress, this attention became magnified as a result of the behavior of overwhelmingly negative private security contractors, which came to be epitomized by Eric Prince and Blackwater USA. On March 31, 2004, four Blackwater personnel were murdered, and their bodies were desecrated and hung from a bridge over the Euphrates River at Fallujah. This event was followed shortly thereafter by a major military operation by the US Marines, who eventually occupied Fallujah at great cost in lives. On September 16, 2007, at Nisour Square, in Baghdad, Blackwater security employees killed seventeen Iraqis and wounded twenty, all unarmed civilians. This massacre came to symbolize the recklessness and impunity of private security contractors.

Analysis

In order to analyze contracting out during the global war on terrorism, in the remainder of this chapter I utilize the framework described in Chapter 1 to organize various sources of information.

Strategy

The titles of two GAO reports, published ten years apart, suggest the implications of the lack of a strategy for both conflicts. The first, published in 2003, is *Military Operations: Contractors Provide Vital Services to Deployed Forces but Are Not Adequately Addressed in DOD Plans*.[32] The second, published in 2013, is *Warfighter Support: DOD Needs Additional Steps to Fully Integrate Operational Contract Support into Contingency Planning*.[33] The implications arising from the lack of integration of operational contract support is captured in the following quote from Secretary of Defense Robert M. Gates: "As the contractor presence developed in Iraq after the original invasion, there was no plan, no structure, no oversight, and no coordination. The contractors' role grew willy-nilly as each U.S. department or agency contracted with them independently, their numbers eventually climbing to some 150,000."[34]

The absence of a strategy in these two conflicts, which resulted in a huge rush to contract out, as Gates writes, "willy-nilly," demands further explanation. The Goldwater-Nichols Defense Reorganization Act of 1986 stipulates that the executive must publish annually a national security strategy (NSS). However, once the rationale of the Cold War disappeared, the urgency and the political implications of publishing an NSS changed. Between 1987 and 2000, a NSS was published every year except in 1989 and 1992. In contrast, during the eight-year George W. Bush and Barack Obama administrations, there were two each. The comments of Robert Gates, upon accepting the offer of the position of secretary of defense from President Bush in October 2006, are telling: "Personally, I don't recall ever reading the president's NSS when preparing to become secretary of defense. Nor did I read any of the previous National Defense Strategy documents when I became secretary. I never felt disadvantaged by not having read these scriptures."[35]

On May 1, 2003, after twenty-six days of combat operations, the United States subdued Iraq, and Saddam Hussein went into hiding. On that same day, President George W. Bush proclaimed "Mission Accomplished" on the aircraft carrier USS *Abraham Lincoln*. There is consensus among virtually all sources consulted—

journalists, RAND Corporation researchers, and ex–Department of Defense policymakers—that the absence of strategy was a, if not the, major factor in the missteps and failures after the initial invasion.[36] In the most succinct summary I have found on the absence of a strategy by President Bush and the war in Iraq, Jean Edward Smith writes:

> The uniformed military and the civilian leadership at the Pentagon had both assumed the Iraqi invasion would be short.... The agreed goal was to leave an Iraq that was whole, was respectful of its minorities, and that would not support terrorism or attack its neighbors. That was what Bush had approved as well.... But on May 1, 2003, the goal had changed. Instead of an early withdrawal, George Bush altered his strategy.... This was a unilateral decision made by the president.... By Bush's order, the United States military moved from being liberators to being occupiers. It was downhill from there.[37]

In short, while there was a strategy for the invasion, there was none after the fall of the Saddam Hussein regime, and there was clearly none regarding the use of contractors to achieve security. For a variety of well-documented reasons, Iraq collapsed into sectarian divisions, extremely high violence, and finally chaos.[38] The same would apply to Afghanistan, only more so. To quote the expert on military history and strategy, Hew Strachan: "Arguably, strategy has been absent throughout the wars in Iraq and Afghanistan. In part this is because the political objects have been unclear, or variable, or defined in terms too broad to be deliverable in strategic terms. Because there has been no clear relationship between the ends and the limited (and often inappropriate) means, strategy is simply not possible."[39]

While the US government produces documents on strategy, when a strategy was indeed necessary in Iraq and Afghanistan, none was forthcoming. Or rather, there were several, but in their totality they were incoherent, and there was no plan available at all to be implemented after the initial invasion. Secretary of Defense James Mattis (January 2017–January 2019), who during his time holding this position did develop a real (as opposed to rhetorical) strategy, states the following in the first two lines of the chapter "Restoring

Our National Security": "For the past twenty years, across administrations of both political parties, the United States has been operating largely unguided by strategy. We have been much too reactive to events and crises, and have allowed others to define the perception and outcomes of our engagement around the world."[40]

With the consensus on the lack of a strategy for what the United States would be facing in Iraq from the invasion in 2003 until at least 2011, or in Afghanistan, America's longest war, 2001 until 2021, we can now examine some of the elements of DoD contractor support.

Adherence to the Federal Acquisition Regulation and Inherently Governmental Function

I believe it is significant that none of the articles on contingency operations in Iraq and Afghanistan, positive, negative, or otherwise, deal with the legal framework whereby DoD awarded the contracts. In the case of these operations, it was the FAR. This may be because the authors are not aware of how the "system" works, since as noted in the introduction to this book, the mechanisms for awarding contracts are dealt with virtually exclusively by acquisition specialists.[41] It may also be because, according to the Commission on Wartime Contracting in Iraq and Afghanistan, the main tenets of the FAR were not implemented in the conflicts in Iraq and Afghanistan. In Chapter 7 of "Transforming Wartime Contracting: Controlling Costs, Reducing Risks," titled "Contract Competition, Management, and Enforcement Are Ineffective," the commission concludes with the following: "Agencies have faced unique challenges in trying to make peacetime practices regarding contract competition, management, and enforcement apply in Iraq and Afghanistan. . . . The need to accomplish missions in Iraq and Afghanistan with constrained resources has led to the award of contracts using procedures that have not resulted in effective competition."[42] The commission noted that the federal procurement system is founded on three fundamental tenets: full and open competition in which all responsible firms are allowed to participate, transparency through public notice of US government requirements and awards, and process integrity that is consistently enforced through policies and laws on ethical behavior, timely audits, and contract oversight. Throughout the chapter the commission documents the lapses and makes a series of recommendations to overcome its conclusion on the topic of competition and management: "The lessons from contingency contracting in Iraq and Afghanistan are that agencies have not effectively employed acquisition-management strategies that balance the United States' interests with contractors' competing objectives."[43]

The commission, in Chapter 2 of the report, "'Inherently Governmental' Rules Do Not Guide Appropriate Use of Contractors in Contingencies," finds that the concept of inherently governmental is, in the commission's terms, not sufficient, and states: "The published guidance reflects much thought and effort. Unfortunately, the overall result is muddled and unclear. It is riddled with exceptions, ambiguities, and ad hoc legislated interventions. The Commission does not consider it a sound platform from which to make risk-based or other decisions, beyond those driven by statutory or policy mandates, on what functions are appropriate to contract."[44] When the commission wrote this, it obviously had the impression that there would be a single definition of what was inherently governmental.[45] However, the political process surrounding the (re)definition of inherently governmental discussed at the beginning of this chapter resulted in, as discussed in the CRS report also cited at the beginning of this chapter, two definitions of inherently governmental functions.[46] If the commission rejected the utility of inherently governmental functions assuming one definition, I can only imagine its reaction to having to base decisions on two definitions.

Education and Training

The focus here is on the problems of insufficient numbers of contracting officers, their distance from the conflicts for which contracts were awarded, and the management of contractors by other contractors. These issues, with particular emphasis on contractors supervising contractors, were dealt with in a recommendation of the commission in the following terms: "Agency heads should: Provide funding and direction to establish a trained, experienced, and deployable cadre for acquisition-management and contractor-oversight functions in areas of contingency operations so that the government has an alternative to relying on contractors for acquisition management and oversight."[47] This recommendation deals with both the number and location of contracting officers. In its report for the secretary of the Army, the Gansler Commission report directly addresses the fact that the contract management workforce has not increased despite a sevenfold increase in the workload.

> In 1990, the Army had approximately 10,000 people in contracting. This was reduced to approximately 5,500, where it has remained relatively constant since 1996.... Yet both the number of contract actions (workload) and the dollar value of procurements (an indicator of complexity) have dramatically increased in the past decade while the contracting workforce has remained constant. The dollar value of Army contracts has increased 331 percent from $23.3 billion in 1992 to $100.6 billion in 2006, while the number of Army contract actions increased 654 percent from approximately 52,900 to 398,700 over the same period.[48]

Furthermore, the overwhelming majority of COs are civilians; according to the Gansler Commission report, out of a total of 5,800, there are only 279 military personnel doing this job.[49] This is an important point, as military personnel can be deployed more easily than can civilians, and the report goes into some detail on why it is difficult to deploy civilians.[50] This means that the COs are not located in Iraq or Afghanistan, where the contracted-out work is being done, but rather in the United States. In his testimony to the Senate Armed Services Committee in early 2009, Gansler noted the sharp decrease in the number of Army general officers involved in acquisitions, from five in 1990 to zero in 2007.[51] This is of fundamental importance because, if there are no general officer positions in the Army Contracting Corps, it cannot attract, much less retain, motivated officers aspiring to advance in rank.[52] The background to this situation is found in the reduction of military forces at the end of the Cold War in the 1990s. While overall US Army forces, for example, were reduced 32 percent from 1990 to 2003, the ranks of COs were reduced 45 percent, from 10,000 to 5,500, including the elimination of all flag and general officer positions during the same period.[53] Unsurprisingly, the rapid ramp-up in US military operations and security contracting in Iraq and Afghanistan led to a shortage of COs to provide oversight of the implementation of the contracts. Another serious issue arises from the fact that DoD has contracted out extensively to oversee its acquisitions processes. In testimony before the House Oversight and Investigations subcommittee, John K. Needham, director of acquisition and sourcing management for the GAO, observed that at the end of fiscal year 2008, the number of civilian and military personnel in DoD's acquisition workforce totaled nearly 126,000, of which civilian personnel constituted 88 percent.[54] As the number of civilian- and military-acquisition personnel declined, DoD outsourced the contracting function to augment the in-house workforce. The GAO found that the number of contract personnel in acquisition-related functions averages 37 percent, with ranges from 22 percent in the Army to 47 percent in joint programs.[55]

Also concerning education and training is a provision regarding education of those who will have to work with contractors. Section 849 in the NDAA for fiscal year 2008 "required DOD, and especially the Army, to train Military personnel who are outside the acquisition workforce but are expected to have acquisition responsibility."[56] The same recommendation was made in the Gansler Commission report. And a CRS report states:

> However, while a number of contracting officers and other acquisition officials are in Iraq, most of DOD's acquisition workforce is generally not deployed or embedded with the military during expeditionary operations. As the number of contractors in the area of operations has increased, the operational force—the service men and women in the field—increasingly rely on, interact with, and are responsible for managing contractors. Yet, a number of military commanders and service members have indicated they did not get adequate information regarding the extent of contractor support in Iraq and did not receive enough pre-deployment training to prepare them to manage or work with contractors.[57]

This issue is important because contractors in contingency operations, and in any context, do not report to the military officers, including operational commanders, but to the firm that was awarded the contract. Therefore, it is important for officers, especially the commanders, to know about care and feeding of contracted personnel. During my research, I learned in September 2009 while conducting interviews at the Office of the Secretary of Defense and J-7, "Education, Training, and Doctrine," of the Joint Chiefs of Staff, that personnel at Joint Forces Command developed an online course of some thirty hours of instruction for use at the war colleges by officers who would be taking command in contingency operations. These courses were never mandated, however, and currently there is at the most only token training or education for incoming military commanders in dealing with contractors on the battlefield.[58] I have sought further information on such possible courses from J-7, Defense Acquisition University, and the Naval and Army War Colleges, and have received no information that they exist. In contrast, my informants, including an instructor teaching on contingency contracting and another who participated in a long report at RAND for DoD that included a recommendation for such education, inform me that either these courses do not exist, or they are simply unaware of any.[59] To the best of my knowledge, Congress did not follow up on this issue.[60]

Implementation

A recommendation of the commission quoted earlier includes both COs who award contracts and those in theater who oversee the implementation, the contracting officer representatives. The recommendation was: "Agency heads should: Provide funding and direction to establish a trained, experienced, and deployable cadre for acquisition-management and contractor-oversight functions in areas of contingency operations so that the government has an alternative to relying on contractors for acquisition management and oversight."[61] While the CO is the only individual authorized to award and make changes to the contract and represent the government in contractual matters, it is the COR who provides technical oversight of the contractor's performance. He or she then provides feedback to the CO.

In testimony to the US House of Representatives, Comptroller General Walker, who was also head of the GAO, went into some detail on CORs in the following terms: "While this [inadequacy of the acquisition workforce, including oversight] is a DOD-wide problem, having too few contract oversight personnel presents unique difficulties at deployed locations, given the more demanding contracting environment as compared to the United States."[62] He reported specifically that the CORs received little pre-deployment training on their roles and responsibilities in monitoring contractor performance. "In most cases, deploying individuals were not informed that they would be performing contracting officer's representative duties until after they had deployed, which hindered the ability of those individuals to effectively manage and oversee contractors."[63]

There is agreement among all sources consulted on the lack of preparation for CORs, and the unreasonable multitasking expected of them. The Gansler report is very critical of the way CORs are used as a mechanism for implementation:

> Contracting Officer's Representatives (CORs), who are an essential part of contract management, are at best a "pick-up game" in-theater. CORs represent the "last tactical mile" of expeditionary contracting. However, CORs are assigned as contract managers/administrators as an "extra duty," requiring no experience. A COR is often a young Soldier who does not have any experience as a COR. . . . Although being a COR would ideally be a career-enhancing duty, the COR assignment is often used to send a young Soldier to the other side of the base when a commander does not want to have to deal with the person. Additionally, little, if any, training is provided. To further compound matters, generally all COR training is geared for a low-operations, low risk tempo, so it is barely adequate. Despite this, there are still too few CORs. Moreover, COR turnover is high, frequently leaving many gaps in contract coverage.[64]

A later study by the special inspector general for Iraq reconstruction (SIGIR) concludes that there are major ongoing problems regarding CORs:

> SIGIR identified vulnerabilities in the government's oversight. Generally, the CORs' experience and training was limited, and they had insufficient time available to devote to their oversight responsibilities. This hampered their ability to perform their oversight responsibilities. For example, of 27 CORs responding to SIGIR questions, only 4 CORs said that they had previous contracting

experience, 11 said that their training was insufficient to meet their job and requirements, and 6 said that other duties prevented them from conducting adequate oversight.[65]

The most recent report from the GAO on private security contractors slams the use of CORs by DoD to oversee contracts.[66]

In terms of preparation to be a COR, the requirements are minimal.[67] Unfortunately, according to the most recent GAO report dealing with the implementation of the commission's recommendations, of September 2021, this item ("Agency heads should: Provide funding and direction to establish a trained, experienced, and deployable cadre for acquisition-management and contractor-oversight functions in areas of contingency operations so that the government has an alternative to relying on contractors for acquisition management and oversight.") is listed as "not implemented."[68]

Oversight by Congress and Its Auditing Institution, the GAO

Most efforts to make outsourcing effective and accountable have been stimulated by the US Congress. According to the May 17, 2013, CRS report: "Many analysts and senior DOD officials have stated that without the efforts of Congress, DOD would not have been as successful at improving operational contract support."[69] Beginning in mid-2004 with hearings conducted by the House Oversight and Government Reform Committee, the antics of Eric Prince and Blackwater USA came to general public attention, stimulating a great deal of very negative media attention. Beginning with the fiscal year 2007 NDAA (the Democrats having won control of Congress in the 2006 elections), Congress gave very specific guidance to DoD to remedy, through a huge variety of initiatives, contingency contracting. The CRS report "Department of Defense's Use of Contractors to Support Military Operations: Background, Analysis, and Issues for Congress," of May 17, 2013, on page 14 reports on twenty-seven of these initiatives between 2007 and the publication of the report.[70]

Congress also created two special, or specifically tasked, inspectors general: special inspector general for Iraq reconstruction (SIGIR)

(2004) and special inspector general for Afghan reconstruction (SIGAR) (2008), primarily to counter widely perceived fraud, waste, and abuse in Iraq and Afghanistan. They were created to report directly to Congress. I was informed by staff at SIGIR that the administration of President George W. Bush attempted to shut down SIGIR five times, but Congress, under the control of the Democrats, did not allow that to happen.[71] According to its final report, during the nine years of SIGIR's operations, SIGIR monitored the expenditure of $60 billion for programs and projects in Iraq, and conducted 220 audits and 170 inspections.[72] SIGAR is auditing the $137 billion appropriated for Afghanistan between 2002 and 2021.[73] Both SIGIR and SIGAR were specialized auditing bodies, built loosely on the model of the GAO, but with remits that extend only to the period until the appropriated funds had been exhausted.

Congress also created and, jointly with the administration of George W. Bush, selected the eight commissioners for the Commission on Wartime Contracting in Iraq and Afghanistan, whose function was to assess contingency contracting in Iraq and Afghanistan. It was created in 2008 (Public Law 110-181) to assess contingency contracting and provide recommendations to Congress. Between 2008 and 2011, the commission and its research team held twenty-five hearings; made twenty trips to Iraq, Afghanistan, and other countries; made sixty-three domestic trips; issued seven interim reports; and released its final report, "Transforming Wartime Contracting: Controlling Costs, Reducing Risks," in August 2011. The final report made fifteen recommendations with relevance to DoD, the Department of State, and USAID.[74]

A year later, in August 2012, at the request of Senators Claire McCaskill and Jim Webb, the GAO issued a report on the degree to which the DoD, the Department of State, and USAID implemented the commission's recommendations.[75] What that report demonstrated, at least to me, was minimal implementation of the recommendations from the commission. Despite that, under the rubric "Agency Comments," the report states: "We requested comments on a draft of this report from DOD, State, and USAID. The three agencies informed us that they had no comments on the draft's findings and provided us with technical comments that we incorporated into the final report as appropriate."[76]

Despite what I construe as critical comments in the CRS and GAO reports after the August 1, 2012, GAO report, there was, to the best of my knowledge, no follow-up until the NDAA for fiscal year 2020, in which Congress directed the GAO to report on contingency contracting (Section 887), including "the implementation of the recommendations made by the Commission" and private security contractors.[77] Whether this inaction was due to lobbying by elements of the industry or not, I am in no position to give an informed opinion. By my reading, the September 2021 GAO report is devastating in its findings regarding implementation of the (now sixteen) recommendations for DoD, in which nine are classified as implemented, two not implemented, and four as challenging to implement. The GAO report found problems mainly in the system for contracts and contractors in contingencies. This is an important point beyond the commission's recommendations pertaining to Iraq and Afghanistan, for it also applies to contractors in the Africa Command (AFRICOM) area of responsibility. In my communications with the GAO in mid-2021, I was informed that these gaps in DoD are important in the decision by the GAO to define DoD contract management as "high risk."[78] The NDAA for fiscal year 2022 specifically refers to the analysis of the September 2021 report (GAO-21-344) and states: "We direct the Secretary of Defense to implement the recommendations of the GAO report and provide a progress briefing to the congressional defense committees not later than July 1, 2022."[79]

Conclusion

There are at least nine books and countless popular and scholarly articles on PSCs. Virtually all the scholarly books on outsourcing in Iraq and Afghanistan scrutinize the conduct of security contractors, as do the more popular printed and online media. Yet, most recently the numbers of the private security contractors dropped precipitously with the departure of US troops from Iraq and the consolidation of bases in Afghanistan before the complete departure of the United States in

August 2021. According to the data provided in the CRS report updated February 22, 2021, pertaining to the fourth quarter of 2020, whereas there were a total of 22,562 contractors in Afghanistan, there were 1,813 security contractors, with only 456 US citizens; for Iraq and Syria the figures were 4,826, of which 2,409 were private security contractors, of which 147 were US citizens.

According to the first line of the executive summary of the final report of the Commission on Wartime Contracting in Iraq and Afghanistan: "At least $31 billion, and possibly as much as $60 billion, has been lost to contract waste and fraud in America's contingency operations in Iraq and Afghanistan."[80] Clearly, the problem of contracting-out in contingency operations in Iraq and Afghanistan cannot be reduced to a focus exclusively on private security contractors.

The analysis in this chapter results in as bleak a description of DoD's experience in contracting-out as in achieving military success in Iraq and Afghanistan. The various fiascos reviewed in this chapter are totally understandable by reading the recommendations of the commission issued in 2012. What is perplexing to me is why the recommendations were never, at least fully, implemented. While I have no insights into the lobbying of the industry, one must be aware that there is a huge amount of money and a great deal of employment related to contracting-out, including in contingency contracting.

In support of my conclusions here, I think it is worth calling attention to Inspector General for Afghanistan Reconstruction John F. Sopko's final report immediately before the ultimate debacle in early August 2021: "In conclusion, this report raises critical questions about the U.S. government's ability to carry out reconstruction efforts on the scale seen in Afghanistan. As an inspector general's office charged with overseeing reconstruction spending in Afghanistan, SIGAR's approach has generally been technical; we identify specific problems and offer specific solutions. However, after 13 years of oversight, the cumulative list of systemic challenges SIGAR and other oversight bodies have identified is staggering."[81] In reaching this wider conclusion on "systemic challenges," Sopko reports he drew on 760 interviews and reviewed thousands of government documents. Of his seven lessons learned, the three that are not specific to Afghanistan and to reconstruction are very similar to those I include in my framework for both Iraq and Afghanistan. The first is the lack of a strategy, and the others, while grouped differently than mine, amount to a lack of oversight, lack of education, and lack of effective means of implementation. He does not mention the legal framework for contracting-out, which was presumably the FAR, nor does he mention the resources, which in the case of SIGAR and Afghanistan reconstruction were $145 billion as of June 2021.

In sum, Sopko, although a lawyer coming from an oversight and accountability background, went far beyond the auditing orientation of the GAO, and SIGAR, to analyze what went wrong in Afghan reconstruction. This broader analysis is what I have attempted in this chapter, and indeed in the whole book.

Notes

1. Commission on Wartime Contracting in Iraq and Afghanistan, "Transforming Wartime Contracting: Controlling Costs, Reducing Risks" (Washington, DC, August, 2011), p. 1. In addition, the final reports of the inspector generals of SIGIR and SIGAR are both enlightening and profoundly disturbing. See "Learning from Iraq," March 2013; "What We Need to Learn: Lessons from Twenty Years of Afghanistan Reconstruction," August 2021, at https://cybercemetery.unt.edu/archive/cwc/20110929213815 and http:/www.wartimecontracting.gov. The final reports from SIGIR and SIGAR are available via Google.

2. The final report of the commission was presented to the Senate Committee on Armed Services on October 19, 2011; https://www.govinfo.gov/content/pkg/CHRG-112shrg72564/pdf/CHRG-112shrg72564.pdf. It was presented by Dov Zakheim, whom I had interviewed during the work of the commission.

3. GAO, "Contingency Contracting: Agency Actions to Address Recommendations by the Commission on Wartime Contracting in Iraq and Afghanistan" (Washington, DC, August 1, 2012), p. 3.

4. GAO, "Contingency Contracting: DOD Has Taken Steps to Address Commission Recommendations, but Should Better Document Progress and Improve Contract Data" (Washington, DC, September 2021), p. 1.

5. I found the DoD inspector general report "Contingency Contracting: A Framework for Reform—2015 Update" particularly interesting.

On the cover page it states: "We are providing this report as an update to re-emphasize the ongoing problems identified in the previous DoD Office of Inspector General Reports." The report goes into detail on a long litany of "Problems in Contingency Contracting Operations." See https://www.dodig.mil/reports.html/Article/1119143/contingency-contracting-a-framework-for-reform-2015-update.

6. See Thomas C. Bruneau, *Patriots for Profit: Contractors and the Military in U.S. National Security* (Stanford: Stanford University Press, 2011), p. 144.

7. Kate M. Manuel, "Definitions of 'Inherently Governmental Function' in Federal Procurement Law and Guidance" (Washington, DC: Congressional Research Service, December 23, 2014). The commission's Chapter 2 is titled "'Inherently Governmental' Rules Do Not Guide Appropriate Use of Contractors in Contingencies." In *Patriots for Profit* I deal extensively with this issue on pp. 156–157, and provide in Appendix 2, pp. 171–178, "Letter to OFPP of OMB, by Contracting Industry Representatives," dated June 8, 2009. This issue will be dealt with later in this chapter.

8. *CRS In Focus*, "A-76 Competitions" (Washington, DC, June 2, 2020).

9. GAO, "Contingency Contracting: DOD Has Taken Steps" (Washington, DC, September 2021), p. 1

10. This table is taken from US Congress, "Contractors' Support of U.S. Operations in Iraq" (Washington, DC: Congressional Budget Office, August 2008), p. 13.

11. Heidi M. Peters, "Department of Defense Contractor and Troop Levels in Afghanistan and Iraq, 2007–2020" (Washington, DC: Congressional Research Service, February 22, 2021), pp. 8, 18, respectively. The report states: "In late 2017, the DOD stopped reporting the number of U.S. military personnel deployed in support of operations in Afghanistan, Iraq, and Syria as part of its quarterly manpower reports and in other official releases" (p. 3).

12. GAO, "Contingency Contracting: DOD Has Taken Steps," p. 2.

13. Singer reviews some of the drawbacks of others' approaches to contracting out: Peter W. Singer, *Corporate Warriors: The Rise of the Privatized Military Industry* (Ithaca: Cornell University Press, 2003), pp. 89–91. The figure is from p. 93, fig. 6.2.

14. Ibid., pp. 91–98.

15. Ibid., p. 97, n. 24.

16. In a survey of 550 firms a team at the Naval Postgraduate School concluded: "This data points clearly to the intermingling of service provisions up and down the spear that Avant and Singer (and others) have remarked on as a characteristic of the sector." Nicholas Dew and Bryan Hudgens, "The Evolving Private Military Sector: A Survey" (Monterey, CA: Naval Postgraduate School, Acquisition Research Program, Graduate

School of Business and Public Policy), http://www.acquisitionsresearch.org. In addition to Singer, the reference is to Avant's diagram on p. 7; Deborah Avant, *Political Institutions and Military Change: Lessons from Peripheral Wars* (Ithaca: Cornell University Press, 1994).

17. GAO, "Warfighter Support: Continued Actions Needed by DOD to Improve and Institutionalize Contractor Support in Contingency Operations" (Washington, DC, March 17, 2010), pp. 3–4; testimony before the Subcommittee on Defense of the House Committee on Appropriations.

18. Karen E. LeDoux, "LOGCAP 101: An Operational Planner's Guide," *Army Logistician* (May–June 2005), p. 27.

19. GAO, "Defense Logistics: High-Level DOD Coordination Is Needed to Further Improve the Management of the Army's LOGCAP Contract" (Washington, DC, March 2005), p. 5. This report provides extensive information on LOGCAP, especially but not limited to the US Army.

20. Ibid., p. 5.

21. LeDoux, "LOGCAP 101," p. 7.

22. GAO, "Defense Logistics," p. 1.

23. Army Sustainment Command, *LOGCAP III Task Order Continues Support in Iraq* (Washington, DC: Office of Public Affairs, May 5, 2010), https://www.army.mil/article/38607/logcap_iii_task_order_continues_support_in_iraq.

24. Army Sustainment Command, *LOGCAP V Performance Contractors Selected* (Washington, DC: Office of Public Affairs, April 15, 2019), https://www.army.mil/article/220353/logcap_v_performance_contractors_selected.

25. Ibid.

26. "Commission on Wartime Contracting in Iraq and Afghanistan," final report, p. 76.

27. John F. Sopko, "Letter to Commanding Generals of U.S. Army Sustainment Command and U.S. Army Contracting Command," September 12, 2014, https://www.sigar.mil/pdf/special%20projects/SIGAR-14-97-SP.pdf.

28. The data for 1990 are from US Department of Defense, "Selected Manpower Statistics Fiscal Year 1990" (Washington, DC: Washington Headquarters Services, Directorate for Information Operations and Reports, Department of Defense). Data for 1997 are found at http://siadapp.dmdc.osd.mil/personnel/MILITARY/history/tab9.

29. US Congress, "Contractors' Support of U.S. Operations in Iraq" (Washington, DC: Congressional Budget Office, August 2008), p. 13. It should also be noted that DoD was the lead agency for postwar Iraq in accord with President George W. Bush's National Security Presidential Directive 24 of January 20, 2003. See Nora Bensahel, "Mission Not Accomplished: What Went Wrong with Iraqi Reconstruction," *Journal of Strategic Studies* 29, no. 3 (June 2006), p. 458.

30. Jennifer K. Elsea et al., "Private Security Contractors in Iraq: Legal Issues" (Washington, DC: Congressional Research Service, September 29, 2008), p. 3.

31. Peters, "Department of Defense Contractor and Troop Levels," pp. 7–16.

32. GAO, "Military Operations: Contractors Provide Vital Services to Deployed Forces but Are Not Adequately Addressed in DOD Plans" (Washington, DC, June 24, 2003).

33. GAO, "Warfighter Support: DOD Needs Additional Steps to Fully Integrate Operational Contract Support into Contingency Planning" (Washington, DC, February 8, 2013).

34. Robert M. Gates, *Duty: Memoirs of a Secretary at War* (New York: Knopf, 2014), p. 224.

35. Ibid., p. 144.

36. The same applies, and even more so, for Afghanistan since resources were redirected from combat there to the invasion of Iraq. Indeed, Brent Scowcroft, who had been national security advisor for Presidents Ford and George H. Bush, as well as chairman of very high-level national security advisory boards, published an editorial in the *Wall Street Journal* on August 15, 2002, in which he advocated a continued focus on Afghanistan and to not invade Iraq. See Nora Bensahel, "Mission Not Accomplished: What Went Wrong with Iraqi Reconstruction," *Journal of Strategic Studies* 29, no. 3 (June 2006); Nora Bensahel, Olga Oliker, Keith Crane, Richard R. Brennan Jr., Heather S. Gregg, Thomas Sullivan, and Andrew Rathmel, *After Saddam: Prewar Planning and the Occupation of Iraq* (Santa Monica: RAND Arroyo Center, 2008). Collins, a DoD official, lists ten "Errors in Decisionmaking and Execution"; Joseph J. Collins, "Choosing War: The Decision to Invade Iraq and Its Aftermath" (Washington, DC: Institute for National Strategic Studies, National Defense University, April 2008), p. 16.

37. Jean Edward Smith, *Bush* (New York: Simon and Schuster, 2016), pp. 477–478.

38. The title of Thomas Ricks's *Fiasco: The American Military Adventure in Iraq* (New York: Penguin, 2006) captures well the chaotic situation in Iraq and the haplessness of US policy in dealing with it, and the book provides details to justify the title.

39. Hew Strachan, *The Direction of War: Contemporary Strategy in Historical Perspective* (Cambridge: Cambridge University Press, 2013), p. 218.

40. James O. Ellis Jr., James N. Mattis, and Kori Schake, "Restoring Our National Security," in George P. Schultz, ed., *Blueprint for America* (Stanford: Hoover Institution, 2016), p. 137.

41. A positive article is C. Anthony Pfaff and Edward Mienie, "Strategic Insights: Five Myths Associated with Employing Private Military

Companies" (Carlisle, PA: US Army War College, April 5, 2019). Two negative assessments are Sean McFate, "America's Addiction to Mercenaries," *The Atlantic*, August 2, 2016; and Renanah Miles Joyce and Brian Blankenship, "'Money as a Weapon System': The Promises and Pitfalls of Foreign Defense Contracting" (Washington, DC: Cato Institute, June 3, 2020). A balanced policy-oriented article also ignores the mechanisms for contracting out: Caroline Batka, Molly Dunigan, and Rachel Burns, "Private Military Contractors' Financial Experiences and Incentives," *Defense & Security Analysis* 36, no. 2 (2020), pp. 161–179. I find it amazing that the huge Costs of War project at the Watson Center, Brown University, which has documents, videos, podcasts, and the like, on contingency contracting, has absolutely nothing on how the contracts resulting in the "costs of war" are awarded. See http://watson.brown.edu/costsofwar.

42. Commission on Wartime Contracting in Iraq and Afghanistan, "Transforming Wartime Contracting" (Washington, DC, September 29, 2011) Chapter 7, "Contract Competition, Management, and Enforcement Are Ineffective," p. 150.

43. Ibid., p. 151.

44. Ibid., pp. 41–42.

45. This is clear from Ibid., p. 43, citing a proposed policy letter from OMB.

46. Kate M. Manuel, "Definition of 'Inherently Governmental Function' in Federal Procurement Law and Guidance" (Washington, DC: Congressional Research Service, December 23, 2014).

47. Commission on Wartime Contracting in Iraq and Afghanistan, "Transforming," p. 52.

48. "Urgent Reform Required: Army Expeditionary Contracting," report of the Commission on Army Acquisition and Program Management in Expeditionary Operations (commonly called the Gansler Commission report), October 31, 2007, p. 30. The commission interviewed or took testimony from approximately 150 practitioners and experts. See also Moshe Schwartz, "Training the Military to Manage Contractors During Expeditionary Operations: Overview and Options for Congress" (Washington, DC: Congressional Research Service, December 17, 2008). He states: "However, while a number of contracting officers and other acquisition officials are in Iraq, most of DOD's acquisition workforce is generally not deployed or embedded with the military during expeditionary operations. As the number of contractors in the area of operations has increased, the operational force—the service men and women in the field—increasingly rely on, interact with, and are responsible for managing contractors. Yet, a number of military commanders and service members have indicated they did not get adequate information regarding the extent of contractor support in Iraq and did not receive

enough pre-deployment training to prepare them to manage or work with contractors"; Schwartz, "Training the Military," p. 3.

49. Gansler Commission report, p. 35, tab. 9. It must be emphasized again that the Army is the executive agent for contracting in Iraq and Afghanistan; p. 19, n. 11. The numbers are not always consistent, depending on the date of acquiring the information on military personnel.

50. Gansler Commission report, pp. 36–37.

51. Jacques S. Gansler, "Acquisition Reform: Achieving 21st Century National Security," testimony before the Senate Armed Services Committee, March 3, 2009, p. 3 table. See also the *Federal News Service* for a transcript of his testimony.

52. I interviewed Gansler on February 23, 2009. He also noted that the Defense Contract Management Agency previously had four general officers, but when I interviewed him, it had none.

53. Gansler Commission report, p. 30.

54. John K. Needham, director of acquisition and sourcing management, "Acquisition Workforce: DOD Can Improve Its Management and Oversight by Tracking Data on Contractor Personnel and Taking Additional Actions," testimony before the Oversight and Investigations Subcommittee of the House Committee on Armed Services, April 28, 2009.

55. Ibid.

56. Schwartz, "Training the Military."

57. Gansler Commission report, p. 21. Schwartz, "Training the Military," p. 3.

58. I am aware of the periodic "Contractor Support of U.S. Operations in the USCENTCOM Area of Responsibility," https://www.acq.osd.mil/log/ps.CENTCOM_reports.html/FY21_4Q_5A_Oct2021.pdf, which includes a rubric for education, but I have no idea whether anything is in fact implemented. I note in the most recent one, April 2022, that under "Training" the subtitle is "Joint Knowledge Online," which refers to several online courses. Reading the most recent GAO report on contingency contracting encourages my skepticism further regarding major improvements. See GAO, "Contingency Contracting: DOD Has Taken Steps to Address Commission Recommendations, but Should Better Document Progress and Improve Contract Data" (Washington, DC, September 2021).

59. The RAND report is Molly Dunigan et al., "Human Capital Needs for the Department of Defense Operational Contract Support: Planning and Integration Workforce" (Santa Monica: RAND, 2017). Chapter 5 is "Closing Gaps: Training." An article in an academic journal deals with the same issue: see Caroline Batka, Molly Dunigan, and Rachel Burns, "Private Military Contractors' Financial Experiences and Incentives," *Defense & Security Analysis* 36, no. 2 (2020), p. 174, for a recommendation.

60. Even though the CRS published a report on this issue. See Schwartz, "Training the Military."

61. Gansler Commission report, p. 52.

62. David M. Walker, "DOD Needs to Reexamine Its Extensive Reliance on Contractors and Continue to Improve Management and Oversight," testimony before the Subcommittee on Readiness of the House Committee on Armed Services, March 11, 2008, p. 16. Walker also refers to the Gansler Commission report, which states "that the Army lacks the leadership and military and civilian personnel to provide sufficient support to either expeditionary or peacetime mission. . . . As we noted in our 2006 report [p. 34], without adequate contract oversight personnel in place to monitor its many contracts in deployed locations such as Iraq, DOD may not be able to obtain reasonable assurance that contractors are meeting their contract requirements efficiently and effectively" (p. 17).

63. Ibid., p. 20.

64. Gansler Commission report, p. 43.

65. SIGIR, "Need to Enhance Oversight of Theater-Wide Internal Security Services Contracts" (Washington, DC, April 24, 2009), p. ii.

66. GAO, "Private Security Contractors: DOD Needs to Better Identify and Monitor Personnel and Contracts" (Washington, DC, July 2021), pp. 27–28.

67. It should be noted that the only training CORs receive is a short online course. As a DoD employee, I was required to complete up to thirty online course modules a year. From my experience and that of others, civilians and officers, the most common goal is to get through these required courses as quickly as possible, and if anything is absorbed it is accidental. My students who had the misfortune to serve as CORs in Iraq and Afghanistan had the same (bad) experience. As acting as a COR is "additional duty," these officers saw no incentive in being CORs.

68. GAO "Contingency Contracting: DOD Has Taken Steps" (Washington, DC, September 2021), p. 11.

69. Moshe Schwartz, "Department of Defense's Use of Contractors to Support Military Operations: Background, Analysis, and Issues for Congress" (Washington, DC: Congressional Research Service, May 17, 2013), p. 13.

70. In Ibid., Appendix C, "Select Legislative History," are three pages of details on the sections of the NDAA between fiscal years 2007 and 2013 dealing with contracting-out.

71. Personal interview with Ginger Cruz, deputy inspector general of SIGIR, February 26, 2009.

72. See SIGIR, "Learning from Iraq: A Final Report of the Special Inspector General for Iraq Reconstruction" (Washington, DC, March 2013).

73. John F. Sopko, "What We Need to Learn: Lessons from Twenty Years of Afghanistan Reconstruction" (Washington, DC, August 2021).

74. See https://cybercemetery.unt.edu/archive/cwc/20110929213815/http://www.wartimecontracting.gov.

75. GAO, "Contingency Contracting: Agency Actions" (Washington, DC, August 1, 2012).

76. Ibid., p. 5.

77. Section 889 of the NDAA for fiscal year 2020.

78. See GAO, "Operational Contract Support: Additional Actions Needed to Manage, Account for, and Vet Defense Contractors in Africa" (Washington, DC, December 17, 2015).

79. Page 210 of 670 of "Joint Explanatory Statement" for the NDAA for fiscal year 2020.

80. Commission on Wartime Contracting in Iraq and Afghanistan, "Transforming Wartime Contracting: Controlling Costs, Reducing Risks" (Washington, DC, August, 2011), p. 1.

81. John F. Sopko, "What We Need to Learn: Lessons from Twenty Years of Afghanistan Reconstruction" (Washington, DC, August 2021), pp. XI–XII, https://www.sigar.mil/interactive-reports/what-we-need-to-learn.

4

Contracting Out Intelligence

THE PREVIOUS CHAPTER ON OPERATIONAL CONTRACT SUPPORT AND private security contractors demonstrated that the problems leading to the designation of DoD's contract management as "high risk" is well justified by the two most recent GAO reports on contingency contracting and the use of private security firms. The global war on terrorism had huge implications for outsourcing intelligence, which was overwhelmingly concerned with bringing in personnel either who already had security clearances or who had been cleared in the past and could quickly obtain the required clearances. Outsourcing in the intelligence community consisted primarily of using contracting firms to hire personnel. This led to major concern in the US Congress and is the subject of reports by the CRS and GAO, as well as others. This issue was, however, resolved. My methodology to reach this conclusion is along the lines of Sherlock Holmes in *The Adventure of Silver Blaze*, in which the telltale fact is that the dog didn't bark. The relevance of this for me is that if a contracting-out problem, in this case outsourcing of personnel, is not, or more accurately, is no longer, a relevant issue, the absence of attention to it is a fact in itself.

General Observations on Intelligence

There are three general observations that must be made regarding the intelligence community. The first is conveyed in the anecdote "those that say don't know, and those that know don't say," which puts into question much of the writing, usually sensational, by those outside the IC on intelligence issues. The fact that no response comes from the IC means absolutely nothing, for any response, positive or negative, could provide information to enemies. Second, one must identify some possible sources to write anything about intelligence. I have identified a few that I consider reliable sources that have been within the IC, or, in the case of the CRS and GAO, able to research on classified issues and publish unclassified reports. And third, in the general literature on intelligence, the focus is most often on the need, and the mechanisms, whereby a society trades a certain amount of accountability, implemented through oversight mechanisms for a certain amount of security. There is a dilemma, even a paradox, in the use of secret intelligence in a democracy. A democracy requires accountability, which in turn requires transparency, but intelligence operates in secret. Societies seek, some more successfully than others, to achieve a balance of these contradictory requirements. There is an extensive amount of literature on this tradeoff, and on the creation and operation of these mechanisms of accountability.[1] My focus here is not the accountability of the IC to democratically elected representatives of the population, or to those they appoint into positions of responsibility in the IC, but rather the accountability of those to whom intelligence is outsourced to the representatives and those they appoint. There is, in short, a double level of accountability. Beyond the inevitable focus on accountability, however, and by including the components of my analytical framework, I seek to understand the problems involved by the IC contracting out. This theme will be revisited in Chapter 5, with the IC confronting the need for new technology in the context of great power competition.

Dimensions of Intelligence

It may be useful first to highlight some of the main elements or dimensions of secret intelligence to better understand what is involved in outsourcing. First are the security clearances, ranging from secret, via top secret and sensitive compartmented information, to codeword, and beyond. It takes at least two years to obtain a clearance at the top secret/sensitive compartmented information level, and not all candidates for clearances are successful. Second is the demonstrated need-to-know, which prevents the transfer of information even among those with the same clearances. Third is the incredible complexity and extent of the IC, its functions and products, in the United States. As Jane Harman writes: "Director of National Intelligence James Clapper once said that 'only one entity in the entire universe' is fully briefed on every American intelligence program: 'That's God.'"[2] Fourth are the unique and expensive facilities, including sensitive compartmented information facilities, secure computer networks, and highly trained and cleared clerical and supervisory personnel. Thus, even though contracting-out in the IC is primarily about bringing in personnel, the facilities within which these personnel work, and those working with them and supervising them, must meet extremely high security standards. There is, then, a very large investment in any firm that seeks to obtain contracts from the IC.

A simple and straightforward statement of the responsibility of the IC is as follows: "The Intelligence Community (IC) is charged with providing insight into actual or potential threats to the U.S. homeland, the American people, and national interests at home and abroad."[3] As such, intelligence is a service. Indeed, in many countries the title of the organizations that conduct the intelligence function is "service." In Lowenthal's book, Chapter 15 is titled "Foreign Intelligence Services"; and, for example, in Russia the successors to the KGB are the External Intelligence Service and Federal Security Service, the successor to Securitate in Romania is the Romanian Intelligence Service, and in Canada the main organization is the Canadian Security Intelligence Service.[4] If there is anything common to the intelligence function in the US intelligence community as well as abroad, it is the famous "intelligence cycle," which Lowenthal comments on: "Although meant to be little more than a quick schematic presentation, this circular representation of the process is rather pervasive."[5] The initial stage in this process in all cases is the definition of requirements for the IC to provide the service necessary to achieve the goals stipulated in the short statement of responsibility that began this paragraph. That is, outsourcing intelligence is essentially contracting out a service.

In the United States the IC is huge, consisting of eighteen separate organizations, of which nine are within DoD. In fiscal year 2020 the appropriation for the IC was $85.5 billion.[6] "All but the topline budget numbers are classified."[7] Most of the funds for the IC are buried in the DoD budget, with lesser sums buried in other agencies such as the Department of State, Department of Justice, and Department of Treasury. One of the main authors on the US intelligence community estimates that the intelligence enterprise employs 200,000 people.[8]

Intelligence is mainly about personnel. In a telephone conversation with one of my contacts in the Central Intelligence Agency (CIA), the intelligence officer stated the following: "Contracting out is mainly about personnel."[9] While I will deal with impediments to outsourcing arising from the predominance of secrecy later in this chapter, it must be emphasized that the service provided by the IC to DoD and other agencies whose mission is responding to "potential threats to the U.S. homeland, the American people, and national interests at home and abroad" is mainly a matter of personnel. The focus on personnel is fundamental in the academic literature on outsourcing of intelligence. This is the case in, for example, an early and critical analysis of personnel issues in a 2014 article by Morten Hansen as well as in a 2019 book on outsourcing by Damien Van Puyvelde.[10] Personnel issues are also the focus of the only Congressional Research Service report on the use of contractors and of the two Government Accountability Office reports on the use of contractors.[11] It should be noted these reports are from 2014 and 2015. Further, it is ironic that an opinion piece by one of the most famous technology gurus on the future use of technology in collection and analysis of secret information states the following: "Intelligence gathering and analysis may cease to be an exclusively, or even primarily, human endeavor, but its ultimate objective will still be to understand human-led governments, societies and militaries. Moreover, humans will bring creativity, empathy, comprehension, and strategic thinking to intelligence that machines are unlikely to match anytime soon."[12] Finally, in the authoritative report on the necessity to adopt the most modern technology for intelligence, the authors begin the analysis of what they term "enablers" by looking to culture—that is, to personnel, what they believe and what they do.[13] In what follows I will first analyze the tremendous outsourcing in the IC after 9/11, and the response to the problems arising from it.

The Intelligence Community at the End of the Cold War

The virtually exclusive focus from the beginning of the modern IC in the National Security Act of 1947 until the end of the Cold War was the Soviet Union and its allies. With the disintegration of the Soviet Union, the main reason for the modern IC disappeared, and, for example, the late Senator Daniel Patrick Moynihan submitted legislation twice to abolish the CIA. It must be recalled that at that time the director of the CIA was also director of the IC, so what applied to the CIA also applied to the IC more generally. As stated in a useful summary of the situation at that time: "The Cold War no longer served as the justification for the CIA's mission and massive budget. 'During the 1990s,' recalled Tenet in 2007, 'the conventional wisdom was that we had won the cold war and it was time to reap the peace dividend.' As a result, the federal government slashed the CIA's budget and workforce."[14] According to testimony of Mark Lowenthal: "The budget was flat in the 1990s, and as Director Tenet pointed out several times, we lost the equivalent of 23,000 positions across the Intelligence Community, either people who were never hired or people who were not backfilled when they left. And so, the net result is a huge loss in manpower."[15]

Beginning of the Global War on Terrorism

With the terrorist attack on 9/11, and the subsequent global war on terrorism, the personnel in the IC had to expand very rapidly. However, two primary limits existed in the immediate aftermath of 9/11 for the IC to recruit and train sufficient personnel to implement the global war on terrorism. In the first place, and as noted early in this chapter, there are rigorous requirements resulting in longtime delays in the background investigations and vetting to obtain the necessary security clearances to recruit applicants; second, once an applicant has entered the training pipeline, the process is long and onerous to deliver an intelligence professional with even a minimal capability as a collector or an analyst. Van Puyvelde summarizes the challenge as follows:

> Following 9/11, the requirements for intelligence products and services dramatically increased as senior officials were expected to

provide a rapid and effective answer to the crisis. However, the scarcity of resources and loss of institutional knowledge caused by the downsizing of the 1990s meant that new challenges could hardly be met by government personnel alone. Hiring freezes and attrition had left the intelligence community severely understaffed.[16]

Outsourcing in the IC and the Resulting Polemic

In this situation, with rapidly expanding personnel demands throughout the IC, including increased demands in the Federal Bureau of Investigation (FBI) and in the new Department of Homeland Security, there was no option but to outsource IC work. According to a source cited by Senator Akaka in a US Senate hearing in 2011, 30 percent of the personnel in the IC were contractors.[17] With this background, especially with several scandals, including Abu Ghraib and the one involving Edward Snowden in 2013, who was a contractor and had a security clearance based on the background investigation done by a contracting firm, the outsourcing of intelligence became a very polemic topic. The overall impression from much of the literature at that time was that a key government function, which is the collection and analysis of secret material, already under suspicion, had been turned over to for-profit private firms that were making huge profits from "the people's money." This impression found documentation in several books and articles, including Tim Shorrock's *Spies for Hire: The Secret World of Intelligence Outsourcing*[18] and the *Washington Post* series "Top Secret America," which was published as a book by prominent journalists Dana Priest and William Arkin.[19] As Damien Van Puyvelde summarizes: "Critics argue that government officials have become captive of private interests. They point out that big companies thrive on government intelligence contracts and waste taxpayers' money."[20] These contracts were for personnel who either already had, or could quickly renew through a polygraph, security clearances. In a great many, but impossible to quantify, cases, these were "excessed" or retired professionals from the IC who were hired as contractors and received much increased salaries than they had previously, not to mention the sums charged by the private, for-profit firms that employed them.

Not only did the theme of personnel, particularly that of awarding contracts to private firms that employed the personnel, get the attention of academics, journalists, and the general public, but it also got the critical attention of the US Congress. The general theme of personnel loomed large in a September 20, 2011, Senate hearing and was the primary focus in a June 18, 2014, Senate hearing.[21] The latter hearing focused on the issue of personnel, necessarily involving contractors, in one of two GAO reports. The report "Civilian Intelligence Community: Additional Actions Needed to Improve Reporting on and Planning for the Use of Contract Personnel" makes clear the importance of an annual inventory of contract personnel and the necessity of utilizing credible categories for the analysis of data.[22]

In the midst of the public polemic, and based on the research in reports by CRS and GAO mandated by Congress, in the Intelligence Authorization Act for fiscal year 2008, Section 307, the Congress "directs the DNI [director of national intelligence] to prepare and submit to the intelligence committees an annual personnel assessment for the IC that assesses the personnel levels for each IC element for the fiscal year following the fiscal year in which the assessment is submitted."[23] This explicit guidance in the report demonstrates that the concern for outsourcing personnel for the IC extended beyond the popular and academic media to government decisionmakers and also introduces what was to become a central actor in all that concerns the IC, which is the director of national intelligence.

Resolution of the Issue of Outsourcing and End of the Polemic

In stark contrast to the topics of the previous chapter—OCS and PSCs in contingency contracting, where problems of all sorts continued right up to and beyond the two extremely critical GAO reports of July and September 2021—the main problem of contracting-out in the IC, which was personnel, is no longer an issue. In order to "prove" this I will cite the conclusions of the thoroughly researched and objective book by Damien Van Puyvelde, *Outsourcing Intelligence: Contractors and Government Accountability* of 2019, and follow the methodology of Sherlock Holmes as described at the beginning of this chapter.

In his book, Van Puyvelde analyzes progress in three areas dealing with outsourcing: reinforcing contract management; defining core government activities; and balancing the role of government employees and contractors in the intelligence workforce. Based on his extensive research using documents and interviews, Van Puyvelde concludes that much was improved in all areas.[24] More specifically, he states the following: "First, the book demonstrates that the government has developed an accountability regime for contractors. Second, the recent history of intelligence shows that officials have adapted this regime when accountability failures became obvious in the mid-2000s."[25]

The IC created the "core contractor personnel" category to define and control contractors directly supporting "core" mission areas. According to Intelligence Community Directive Number 612, "Part D Policy," effective October 30, 2009, core contract personnel cannot engage in inherently governmental activities regardless of how defined.[26] They are retained and used by IC elements for the following very specific reasons: immediate surge capacity, discrete nonrecurring tasks, unique experience, specified service, insufficient staffing resources, and transfer of institutional knowledge. The directive stipulates procedures for hiring and remuneration, and encourages the hiring of federal civilian annuitants under different authorities rather than as contractors.[27] This is an annual inventory aligned with the annual *Congressional Budget Justification Book* and provides credible insights into the total core contract workforce.

As I am aware of closed hearings in Congress and from my personal experience at the ODNI, where everything imaginable is classified, I cannot say for certain that the contractor issue, or outsourcing in the IC, is resolved, and that accountability of contractors to government employees is no longer an issue. However, and in line with the concept of the dog that didn't bark, all evidence, or lack of same, points to the conclusion that contracting-out of personnel is no longer an issue. The evidence for this conclusion is substantial.

In the Intelligence Authorization Acts between 2009 and 2021 there is no mention of contracting out personnel issues. There has been no CRS report on contractors since August 18, 2015, and no

GAO report on the IC since February 2014. Of the 170 CRS reports found on the Federation of American Scientists website under the category of "Intelligence Policy," only one, that by Elaine L. Halchin, published in 2015, deals with outsourcing.[28] This lack of focus on personnel issues is particularly dramatic in the CRS report highlighting cross-cutting issues. The only possible personnel issue is diversity, which is also highlighted in several of the Intelligence Authorization Acts, and this concern has resulted in programs, including funding for colleges and universities, to recruit minorities.[29] The most recent critique of outsourcing is Shorrock's article in 2016.[30] Nor, it must be noted, is there a chapter on outsourcing in the fifteen chapters of the eighth edition of Mark Lowenthal's authoritative book.

In short, the main issue, or problem, in outsourcing in the IC in the aftermath of 9/11 was the outsourcing of personnel. It has been resolved to the point that it is no longer a focus of anyone: academics, journalists, or the US Congress.[31]

Analysis of Contracting-Out in the IC in Terms of Framework

In order to explain why outsourcing in the IC is no longer a problem, while it clearly remains the main issues of contingency contracting, I will present material in line with the framework described in the introduction to this book.

Strategy

In fact, as a service, the IC cannot have its own strategy. As stated in the national intelligence strategy (NIS) for 2019: "It [the NIS] supports the national security priorities outlined in the National Security Strategy as well as other national strategies. In executing the NIS, all IC activities must be responsive to national security priorities and must comply with the Constitution, applicable laws and statutes, and Congressional oversight requirements."[32] I see the NISs, which are issued by the ODNI, mainly in terms of communicating the basics of the intelligence function and the main entities involved. Since the overall budget of the IC is on the order of $80 billion a year, some publicity is probably a good thing. The IC provides information and analysis to decisionmakers, civilian and military, whose responsibility it is to implement a strategy, should there be one. That is the main point about the intelligence cycle; the decisionmakers determine the requirements, and the IC provides information and analysis in line with those requirements. There are two large issues in the scholarly literature on intelligence. One is whether decisionmakers act in accord with evidence, and possibly recommendations, of the IC. Another is whether so-called intelligence failures are failures due to poor intelligence or to the unwillingness of decisionmakers, military and civilian, for a great variety of reasons, to follow a particular line of action in accord with intelligence.[33] In the US political system, with eighteen separate intelligence agencies or departments within other agencies providing intelligence, even with "intelligence fusing" a decisionmaker can pick and choose the intelligence product he or she prefers.

The Federal Acquisition Regulation

A founding component of the FAR is the Competition in Contracting Act (CICA) of 1984. There are seven statutory exceptions to the requirement for full and open competition in CICA, and thus to the FAR, and one of them is national security. Due to this exception, the IC is not bound by the FAR requirement of full and open competition.[34] In line with this exception the IC, in September 1999, was engaging with startups and others in Silicon Valley for new technologies, primarily in cyber. In his book, Damien Van Puyvelde discusses In-Q-Tel in terms of a way to harness the information technology (IT) revolution in the face of, as he puts it, "the growth of government acquisition regulations in the second half of the twentieth century," which "progressively complicated the procurement process and scared innovative companies away from the government.... To maintain its leadership, the community would have to reconsider its relationship with the private sector and develop more effective ways to influence and tap into commercial capabilities."[35] A mechanism to tap into these commercial capabilities was the creation of In-Q-Tel. Here I draw on the more or less official description by Rick E. Yannuzzi of the founding and operation of the organization.[36] It was established as an independent nonprofit corporation with offices at the CIA in Langley, Virginia, and in Menlo Park, California. Its mission is to foster the development of new and emerging information technologies and to pursue research and development that produce solutions to the most difficult IT problems facing the IC. To accomplish this, it networks with industry, the venture capital community, academia, and others who are at the forefront of IT innovation. "Through the business relationships that it establishes, In-Q-Tel creates environments for collaboration, product demonstration, prototyping, and evaluations. From these activities flow the IT solutions that the Agency seeks and most importantly, the commercial opportunities for product development by its partners."[37] According to Van Puyvelde and other sources I have consulted, the model has been successfully bringing in new technology.[38]

While Van Puyvelde is clearly aware that In-Q-Tel's status is somewhat anomalous, both Wendy Molzahn and Jon Michaels, whose articles are listed in endnote 38, stress just how unique it is. The former states: "The CIA's contracts with In-Q-Tel are based on the FAR, although the Agency relied on Section 8 of the CIA Act of 1949 to waive certain provisions that otherwise would have applied."[39] Michaels's whole focus in his article is why would the executive branch of the US government allow the degree of autonomy illustrated by In-Q-Tel. He depicts its autonomy as follows:

> The CIA is as free from administrative law constraints as a government agency can be. Its budget is classified and highly discretionary, its operations are beyond public (and often judicial and congressional) scrutiny, and it can fire employees for any reasons short of discrimination based on unconstitutional considerations. The Agency further enjoys incomparable discretion to wheel and deal on the private market. The CIA can establish shady front operations, procure goods and services unburdened by the onerous Federal Acquisition Regulation ... and enter into secret personnel contracts that are unenforceable in court."[40]

It is ironic that Molzahn would like to see DoD follow the model of In-Q-Tel, for we shall see in Chapter 5 that there are currently recommendations for the IC to follow a more recent (Defense

Innovation Unit in 2015) lead taken by DoD in adopting more flexibility in acquisitions.

Education and Training

Between the creation of the "core contract personnel" category in 2009 and today, the focus on personnel issues in the Intelligence Authorization Acts is on hiring, opportunities for education, and diversity.[41] These personnel issues, all basically about diversity, also loom large in the April 12, 2016, CRS report "The U.S. Intelligence Community: Selected Cross-Cutting Issues," where diversity is one of eight issues analyzed, covering five pages, and in the House Permanent Select Committee on Intelligence, where the recommendation to "get the people right" is one of five recommendations, covering six pages.[42] There is also a GAO report on one of the major programs to promote the desired diversity.[43]

In line with the various proposals and recommendations emerging from one or another element of the US Congress, the ODNI has promoted research and publications documenting progress toward the various recommendations, again mainly about diversity.[44]

Congress

Historically, the greatest innovation in the relationship of the IC to the US government was the creation of the two congressional select committees in the mid-1970s specifically intended to conduct oversight. They are the Senate Select Committee on Intelligence and the House Permanent Select Committee on Intelligence. The CRS report "Congressional Oversight of Intelligence: Background and Selected Options for Further Reform" of December 4, 2018, states: "These committees became the model for a permanent oversight framework that could hold the intelligence community accountable for spending appropriated funds legally and ethically and in support of identifiable national security objectives."[45]

The terrorist attack of September 11, 2001, and the 9/11 Commission, created on November 27, 2002, provided the impetus for major change in all aspects of the IC. In the aftermath of the attack, it was clear to everyone that something serious had to be done to prevent another attack, and effective intelligence was at the center of the concern. The 9/11 Commission report outlines the emergence of terrorist threats to the United States and describes the fecklessness of the government's response to the emerging threats. In line with the commission's analysis of the problems with US intelligence, the report's final chapter is titled "How to Do It? A Different Way of Organizing the Government." The commission report makes several specific recommendations for intelligence reform, most of which were included in the Intelligence Reform and Terrorism Prevention Act of 2004.

In view of the complicated politics involved, which, in leading up to the terrorist attack, both exacerbated the lack of cooperation among the agencies and promoted general inertia, the fact that the recommendations were passed into law, and to a high degree implemented, is significant. Kenneth Kitts, in his analysis of several commissions, writes that this was the "most important commission in U.S. history."[46]

The fact of 9/11, as captured in vivid and gruesome detail in the 9/11 Commission report, galvanized Congress to become extremely active in all that concerns intelligence. This is of course manifested first by the Intelligence Reform and Terrorism Prevention Act of 2004.[47] Going beyond legislating, Congress also very substantially increased the budget for intelligence. Whereas the total appropriation authorized by Congress for intelligence in fiscal year 2006 was $43.5 billion, it appropriated $85.8 billion for fiscal year 2020.[48] And, for the third legislative function, oversight, Congress has requested a great many reports by the Congressional Research Service on all aspects of the IC. In line with my counting on the Federation of American Scholars website, there are 170 of these.[49] One of the early reports was on the status of the implementation of the 9/11 Commission report.[50]

A contact of mine in the Central Intelligence Agency called attention to two ongoing reasons, beyond what some have termed "intelligence failures," for congressional attention to the IC. One is the requirement in the legislation for members of Congress to be informed of covert action. In passing, it should be noted that the action to capture or kill Osama bin Laden was considered a covert action, thus the responsibility of the IC, specifically the CIA in this case, under US Code 51.[51] The other is the legal requirement to include in the Intelligence Authorization Act supplemental funds for contract employees.

In sum, the US Congress is very much engaged through its responsibilities in policy, budgets, and oversight with the IC. The main issue in outsourcing in the global war on terrorism was personnel. Through its involvement in all three of its responsibilities, that issue was resolved. A key component of that resolution was the creation of the Office of the Director of National Intelligence.

Implementation

In the Intelligence Reform and Terrorism Prevention Act, Congress eliminated the position of the director of central intelligence and made the director of national intelligence manager of the IC and principal advisor to the president, leaving only the leadership of the CIA to the director of the CIA. This change was extremely important, as Amy Zegart, among others, identified a critical weakness of the bureaucracy based on the National Security Act of 1947:

> The Central Intelligence Agency never succeeded in centralizing intelligence. Instead of exerting discipline over the far-flung intelligence community, the CIA only added to the crowd, producing its own reports and developing its own independent collection capabilities. In addition, the agency pursued a series of illegal and quasi-legal activities that eventually triggered citizen outcries and congressional intervention.[52]

The Intelligence Reform and Terrorism Prevention Act also created the Office of the Director of National Intelligence, an office of approximately 1,500 IC professionals including contractors and employees of other agencies detailed to the ODNI. The CRS report "The Director of National Intelligence" states: "The ODNI enables the DNI to facilitate integration of intelligence collection and analysis, information and intelligence sharing, and budgeting and execution across the other 16 IC components."[53] Initially, with its creation in the Intelligence Reform and Terrorism Prevention Act in 2004, there were criticisms that the ODNI was simply one more level of bureaucracy, and that without budget authority over the whole IC, it was a hollow bureaucracy at that.[54] Based on my research, however, at a minimum the DNI, and the organization of the ODNI, have had at least two positive results. One is to provide coordination throughout the huge IC, which was not possible when the director of the CIA was also director of the IC, and the second is that the DNI has real personnel management authority that is exercised throughout the IC, particularly during the long tenure, 2010–2017, of Lieutenant General James Clapper. As one of my informants stated: "The DNI can and does set up policies for agencies to follow."[55] In short, the DNI emphasized the importance of personnel issues caused by the global war on terrorism and has largely resolved them.[56]

Conclusion

Intelligence must be conceptualized as a service. At the end of the Cold War, and after 9/11, outsourcing of this service meant rapidly increasing personnel. Mainly due to the need for access to secret information requiring security clearances, the tremendous ramp-up was in contracting personnel who already possessed clearances or had and could be quickly updated by polygraph. With the founding of the ODNI, the ongoing support of Congress, and the creation of "core contract personnel," the IC could bring in contract personnel for very specific functions. The core contract personnel are prohibited from engaging in inherently governmental functions. That issue, thusly, was largely resolved. Yet there remained several other issues, mainly concerning the diversification of personnel working in the IC. These issues have been taken on by the ODNI, which issues reports on the status of these diversity issues, and the select congressional oversight committees continue to prioritize these issues of diversity.[57]

Notes

1. For the United States, Lowenthal has a full chapter on mechanisms of oversight and accountability including the executive, legislative, and judicial branches of government, as well as an extensive bibliography for further

reading; Mark M. Lowenthal, *Intelligence: From Secrets to Policy*, 8th ed. (Thousand Oaks, CA: Sage, 2020). The credibility of the author is unquestioned, as he had a long history in the CIA, Department of State, and House of Representatives, and was founder and president of the Intelligence and Security Academy, which offers courses and consults on intelligence and other national security issues. In addition to Lowenthal, for detailed descriptions of the IC, see Office of the Director of National Intelligence, *U.S. National Intelligence: An Overview*, 2013, https://www.dni.gov/files/documents/USNI%202013%20Overview_web.pdf.

2. Jane Harman, "Preface: Why Intelligence Oversight Matters," in Zachary K. Goldman and Samuel J. Rascoff, eds., *Global Intelligence Oversight: Governing Security in the Twenty-First Century* (New York: Oxford University Press, 2016), p. xiii. Jane Harman was Ranking Democrat on the House Permanent Select Committee on Intelligence from 2002 to 2006, and at time of writing, director, president, and CEO of the Woodrow Wilson International Center for Scholars in Washington, DC.

3. *CRS In Focus*, "Defense Primer: National and Defense Intelligence" (Washington, DC, December 30, 2020).

4. Lowenthal, *Intelligence*, chap. 15.

5. Ibid., p. 78. Lowenthal elaborates on the cycle on pp. 78–80, and on p. 81 provides references on the cycle by several international experts on intelligence.

6. *CRS In Focus*, "Defense Primer: Under Secretary of Defense for Intelligence and Security" (Washington, DC, December 30, 2020).

7. Michael E. DeVine, "Intelligence Community Spending: Trends and Issues" (Washington, DC: Congressional Research Service, June 18, 2018), p. 5. In Appendix B, pp. 15–17, DeVine describes the different organizations in the IC that receive the funds and their specific functions: "Since 1952 the intelligence budget has been placed entirely within the defense appropriation under the belief that intelligence programs under the Department of State appropriation were more difficult to shield from cuts." See also Michael E. DeVine, "Congressional Oversight of Intelligence: Background and Selected Options for Further Reform" (Washington, DC: Congressional Research Service, December 4, 2018), pp. 13–14.

8. Loch K. Johnson, *National Security Intelligence: Secret Operations in Defense of the Democracies*, 2nd ed. (Cambridge: Polity, 2017), p. 217, n. 12. Johnson draws on a statement by Admiral Dennis Blair, director of national intelligence, on September 15, 2009.

9. Interview with a longtime employee of the CIA, January 3, 2021.

10. Morten Hansen, "Intelligence Contracting: On the Motivations, Interests, and Capabilities of Core Personnel Contractors in the US Intelligence Community," *Intelligence and National Security* 29, no. 1 (2014): pp. 58–81. Damien Van Puyvelde, *Outsourcing US Intelligence:*

Contractors and Government Accountability (Glasgow: Edinburgh University Press, 2019).

11. Elaine L. Halchin, "The Intelligence Community and Its Use of Contractors: Congressional Oversight Issues" (Washington, DC: Congressional Research Service, August 18, 2015); GAO, "Civilian Intelligence Community: Additional Actions Needed to Improve Reporting on and Planning for the Use of Contract Personnel" (Washington, DC: Government Accountability Office, January 2014); GAO, "Civilian Intelligence Community: Additional Actions Needed to Improve Reporting on and Planning for the Use of Contract Personnel" (Washington, DC: Government Accountability Office, February 13, 2014).

12. Anthony Vinci, "The Coming Revolution in Intelligence Affairs," *Foreign Affairs* (September–October 2010).

13. CSIS, "Maintaining the Intelligence Edge: Reimagining and Reinventing Intelligence Through Innovation" (Washington, DC, January 2021).

14. John T. Reinert, "In-Q-Tel: The Central Intelligence Agency as Venture Capitalist," *Northwestern Journal of International Law & Business* 33, no. 3 (Spring 2013), p. 685.

15. "Intelligence Community Contractors: Are We Striking the Right Balance?" hearing before the Oversight of Government Management, the Federal Workforce, and the District of Colombia Subcommittee of the Senate Committee on Homeland Security and Governmental Affairs, September 20, 2011.

16. Van Puyvelde, *Outsourcing US Intelligence*, p. 87.

17. "Intelligence Community Contractors."

18. Tim Shorrock, *Spies for Hire: The Secret World of Intelligence Outsourcing* (New York: Simon and Schuster, 2008).

19. Dana Priest and William Arkin, *Top Secret America: The Rise of the New American Security State* (New York: Little, Brown, 2011). In addition to these two books—Shorrock and Priest & Arkin—there was also Glenn I. Voelz, *Managing the Private Spies: The Use of Commercial Augmentation for Intelligence Operations* (Seattle: Create Space, 2006), and there were at least eleven of what I would consider serious academic articles. One, by a well-known academic, Simon Chesterman, has the evocative title regarding contracting out: "'We Can't Spy . . . If We Can't Buy': The Privatization of Intelligence and the Limits of Outsourcing 'Inherently Governmental Functions,'" *European Journal of International Law* 19, no. 5 (2008), pp. 1055–1074.

20. Van Puyvelde, *Outsourcing US Intelligence*, p. 6.

21. "Intelligence Community Contractors: Are We Striking the Right Balance?" hearing before the Oversight of Government Management, the Federal Workforce, and the District of Colombia Subcommittee of the

Senate Committee on Homeland Security and Governmental Affairs, September 20, 2011; "The Intelligence Community: Keeping Watch Over Its Contractor Workforce," hearing before the Senate Committee on Homeland Security and Governmental Affairs, June 18, 2014.

22. GAO, "Civilian Intelligence Community: Additional Actions Needed to Improve Reporting on and Planning for the Use of Contract Personnel" (Washington, DC, January 2014). The third, and last, GAO report on the IC is a testimony before the Senate Committee on Homeland Security and Governmental Affairs on February 13, 2014, by Timothy J. DiNapoli, director of acquisition and sourcing management, precisely on the same topic.

23. See https://www.congress.gov/bill/110th-congress/house-bill/2082. The topic of the creation of the DNI will be dealt with later in this chapter.

24. Van Puyvelde, *Outsourcing US Intelligence*, pp. 180–183.

25. Ibid., p. 226.

26. Hansen, "Intelligence Contracting," pp. 58–81, provides a useful analytical approach to the creation of the core personnel contractor position. He is in agreement with my argument in Chapter 3 in stating: "The recently issued new policy in 'inherently governmental functions' . . . still leaves much to be desired in the way of clarification" (p. 80, n. 102).

27. This directive is extremely precise and specific. See Intelligence Community Directive 612.

28. See https://fas.org/sgp/crs/intel/index.html. See also Elaine L. Halchin, "The Intelligence Community and Its Use of Contractors: Congressional Oversight Issues" (Washington, DC, August 18, 2015). The main points are consistent with my argument in this chapter. Halchin focuses only on the lack of expertise by government officials in managing contractors. No other issues concerning outsourcing are discussed.

29. Anne Daugherty Miles, "The U.S. Intelligence Community: Selected Cross-Cutting Issues" (Washington, DC: Congressional Research Service, April 12, 2016).

30. Tim Shorrock, "Five Corporations Now Dominate Our Privatized Intelligence Industry," *The Atlantic*, September 8, 2016.

31. Just to be sure, I contacted personnel at GAO on November 31, 2021, and was informed that there are no reports planned or requested on the topic of IC personnel.

32. See https://www.dni.gov/files/ODNI/documents/National_Intelligence_Strategy_2019.pdf.

33. On these issues, see Lowenthal, *Intelligence*, chap. 9, pp. 253–275. For a review of these issues and a comparative analysis based on secret attacks on Pearl Harbor and Midway, see Erik J. Dahl, "Why Won't They Listen? Comparing Receptivity Toward Intelligence at Pearl Harbor and Midway," *Intelligence and National Security* 28, no. 1 (2013), pp. 68–90.

34. GAO, "Defense Contracting: Improved Policies and Tools Could Help Increase Competition on DOD's National Security Exception Procurements" (Washington, DC, January 2012).

35. Van Puyvelde, *Outsourcing US Intelligence*, p. 81.

36. Rick Yannuzzi, "In-Q-Tel: A New Partnership Between the CIA and the Private Sector" (Langley, VA: Defence Intelligence Journal, 2000).

37. Ibid., p. 2.

38. In addition to Van Puyvelde and Yannuzzi, I have drawn upon the In-Q-Tel website and the following articles: Wendy Molzahn, "The CIA's In-Q-Tel Model: Its Applicability," *Acquisition Review Quarterly* (Winter 2003), pp. 47–61; John T. Reinert, "In-Q-Tel: The Central Intelligence Agency as Venture Capitalist," *Northwestern Journal of International Law & Business* 33, no. 3 (Spring 2013), pp. 677–709; Jon D. Michaels, "The (Willingly) Fettered Executive: Presidential Spinoffs in National Security Domains and Beyond," *Virginia Law Review* 97, no. 4 (May 2011), pp. 801–898.

39. Molzahn, "The CIA's In-Q-Tel Model," p. 57.

40. Michaels, "The (Willingly) Fettered Executive," p. 806.

41. I personally reviewed these acts in detail for the period 2007–2021.

42. Miles, "The U.S. Intelligence Community"; House Permanent Select Committee on Intelligence, https://www.google.com/search?client=safari&rls=en&q=Reconfiguring+to+win+the+innovation+race+in+the+intelligence+community&ie=UTF-8&oe=UTF-8.

43. For a description and analysis of the program intended to diversify personnel in the IC, see Brian M. Mazanec, "Intelligence Community: Actions Need to Improve Planning and Oversight of the Center for Academic Excellence Program" (Washington, DC: Government Accountability Office, August 1, 2019).

44. See, for example, ODNI, *Annual Demographic Report, Fiscal Year 2018*, https://www.dni.gov/index.php/newsroom/reports-publications/reports-publications-2018.

45. Michael E. DeVine, "Congressional Oversight of Intelligence: Background and Selected Options for Further Reform" (Washington, DC: Congressional Research Service, December 4, 2018), p. 3.

46. Kenneth Kitts, *Presidential Commissions and National Security: The Politics of Damage Control* (Boulder: Lynne Rienner, 2006), p. 140. See also "Piloting a Bipartisan Ship: Strategies and Tactics of the 9/11 Commission" (Cambridge: Kennedy School of Government Case Program, 2005). The Intelligence Reform and Terrorism Prevention Act, Public Law 108-458, December 17, 2004, can be found through Google. For implementation, see Richard F. Grimmett, "9/11 Commission Recommendations: Implementation Status" (Washington, DC: Congressional Research Service, December 4, 2006).

47. Intelligence Reform and Terrorism Prevention Act of 2004.

48. The former figure is from the *New York Times* of October 31, 2007, and the latter is from *CRS In Focus*, "Defense Primer."
49. See https://fas.org/sgp/crs/intel/index.html.
50. Grimmett, "9/11 Commission Recommendations."
51. See John Rollins, "Osama bin Laden's Death: Implications and Considerations" (Washington, DC: Congressional Research Service, May 5, 2011).
52. Amy B. Zegart, *Flawed by Design: The Evolution of the CIA, JCS, and NSC* (Stanford: Stanford University Press, 1999), p. 11. Her analysis of the fiasco leading up to 9/11 is required reading for anyone interested in US intelligence: Amy Zegart, *Spying Blind: The CIA, the FBI, and the Origins of 9/11* (Princeton: Princeton University Press, 2007).
53. *CRS In Focus*, "The Director of National Intelligence (DNI)" (Washington, DC, June 7, 2021), provides useful information on the DNI. After the following short heading: "Pursuant to IRTPA, as amended and codified in 50 U.S.C. # 3024, and Executive Order 12333 (as amended, DNI responsibilities include)," then are listed seven responsibilities and sixteen authorities enumerated.
54. Among other criticism, see, for example, from May 3, 2020, https://thehill.com/opinion/national-security/485416-is-it-even-worth-having-a-director-of-national-intelligence.
55. Email response to Bruneau from longtime member of the IC, January 1, 2021.
56. The ODNI, specifically the Chief Human Capital Office, drew on the RAND Corporation to develop the workforce plan, and the role of core contract personnel in it. See Charles Nemfakos et al., "Workforce Planning in the Intelligence Community: A Retrospective" (Santa Monica: RAND, 2013).
57. Diversity in the IC extends to recruiting personnel from other cultures who speak other languages, as all that the IC does concerns other countries and cultures.

5

Facing Great Power Competition

IN RESEARCHING AND WRITING ON CIVIL-MILITARY RELATIONS IN NEW and established democracies, I have found one of the most common and serious problems in analysis is the extreme looseness in use of the concept "strategy." I believe that Gaddis, in the quote early in Chapter 1 of this book, had it right.[1] In practice with most governments and militaries I have found that the term "strategy" is given to almost anything that is written, often with lots of photos of military equipment (most often imported) and of personnel (with females in very trendy uniforms). Most often these "strategies," which are also termed "white books," are "coffee table" tomes, which are useful for the pictures but not much more. And, as noted earlier in this book, lest the reader assume that the United States, in terms of the Goldwater-Nichols Defense Reform Act of 1986, is different, one only need recall that the requirement of a national strategy document annually has been followed more in the breech than in fact with Presidents George W. Bush and Barack Obama producing two during their eight-year terms of office and President Donald Trump one.

About Strategy

In order to remedy this problem, at least in terms of analysis if not policy, I have developed four categories for identifying and presenting information that can amount to what I would term a "strategy."

These four are based on what I have learned through two decades of experience, including responses while lecturing on "strategy" and research in the United States and abroad. The first is whether the document is more or less in synch with the roles and missions that are, or realistically could be, implemented by the military. The second is whether they are elaborated involving branches of government beyond the defense ministry (in DoD). This is relevant because all contemporary military roles and missions necessitate interagency cooperation. The third is whether they are somehow linked to funding sources so that they can in fact be implemented. And the fourth is whether the strategy is disseminated, sooner or later, beyond the limits of the defense and security community to the general population, academia, think tanks, and the like, in order to stimulate popular interest and involvement.[2]

The National Defense Strategy of 2018

My purpose in reviewing these four categories here is to demonstrate that the national defense strategy of January 2018 is indeed a strategy. First, from at least November 2014 during the administration of President Barack Obama in the third offset strategy, the focus of DoD and the US armed forces became "ensuring the ability of the United States to project military power in the face of an emergent suite of advanced military capabilities developed, deployed, and potentially sold by China, Russia, and others."[3] In the third offset strategy the US government defined the contemporary era as one of great power competition, thereby signaling a transition away from the global war on terrorism. In the unclassified summary of the national defense strategy of 2018, the key emphasis is on "the strategic environment in which the United States must operate is one characterized by the erosion of the rules-based international order, which has produced a degree of strategic complexity and volatility not seen 'in recent memory.'" As a result, the document argues, the United States must bolster its competitive military advantage that the national defense strategy views as having eroded in recent decades—relative to the threats posed by China and Russia. It further maintains that "inter-state strategic competition, not terrorism, is the primary concern in U.S. national security." Given that the United States remains a global power, and that, according to the World Bank, it commits 3.7 percent of its gross demestic product, or $778 billion in 2020, to national security and defense, the strategy is indeed feasible.[4]

Second, the national defense strategy of 2018 was developed in an iterative process involving Secretary of Defense General James Mattis (US Marine Corps, retired), the Office of the Under Secretary of Defense for Policy, and the National Security Council (NSC). The national security advisor at that time was Lieutenant General H. R. McMaster (US Army), and the NSC's main role was to coordinate the interagency process. My main source on this issue, a very senior naval officer working closely with Secretary of Defense Mattis, assured me that the national defense strategy was fully coordinated with other branches of government.

Third, Congress has long been concerned with the general theme of great power competition. For example, the Congressional Research Service publishes, approximately twice a year, an analysis of the status of great power competition in the series "Renewed Great Power Competition: Implications for Defense-Issues for Congress."[5] The Congressional Research Service also researches and publishes two other series devoted to the issues of the international security environment and the defense posture of the United States. These are "A Shift in the International Security Environment: Potential Implications for Defense—Issues for Congress" and "U.S. Role in the World: Background and Issues for Congress." In short, even during the global war on terrorism, members of Congress were concerned with the role of the United States in the world beyond the threat of terrorism.

The national defense strategy of 2018, which is the first national defense strategy published in ten years, is mandated by the fiscal year 2017 NDAA mandating that the national defense strategy replace the *Quadrennial Defense Review*, and Congress also rewrote the requirements for DoD strategy documents. Specifically, the NDAA amended legislation "to require the Secretary of Defense to produce a [national defense strategy] which articulates how the Department of Defense will advance U.S. objectives."[6] The national defense strategy is intended by Congress to articulate the overall strategic rationale for programs and priorities. Congress also created a National Defense Strategy Commission, the members of which were appointed by Congress, to assess and evaluate the national defense strategy. The Commission produced *Providing for the Common Defense: The Assessment and Recommendations of the National Defense Strategy Commission*.[7] The Congressional Research Service utilized the report of the National Defense Strategy Commission (the introduction to the strategy is unclassified) to publish a report on the strategy.[8] In short, Congress mandated the creation and was heavily engaged in the assessment of the strategy by the commission. The 2020 NDAA, Section 1708, directs the secretary of defense to report on the implementation of the national defense strategy.[9]

Fourth, leading up to the publication of the national defense strategy of 2018, there was no process of public engagement. There are two relevant facts to be noted here. First, the inspiration of the strategy is found in a chapter in a book written by General Mattis and colleagues, published in 2016. In "Restoring Our National Security" one can find the main themes of the national defense strategy, and the justification for a new strategy.[10] Second, as one of those closely involved in the development of the strategy told me, the public event led by Secretary of Defense Mattis at the Johns Hopkins School for Advanced International Studies on January 19, 2018, was the publicity for the national defense strategy. As noted, the implementing legislation required the review of the strategy by a National Defense Strategy Commission, composed of twelve prominent retired senior officers and civilians, most of whom are currently active in think tanks, NGOs, and academic programs. The Commission brought a high level of prominence to the national defense strategy, its strengths and weaknesses. One of the members of the commission informed me that while the commission had discussed a publicity campaign, for "bureaucratic and personnel reasons" this did not take place. While there was little or no publicity surrounding the launching of the national defense strategy of 2018, it is almost impossible to read anything in the daily *Early Bird* that doesn't deal in one way or another with the themes of the strategy, to include China, Russia, Iran, and North Korea as potential aggressors.

The armed forces of the United States are in fact reorienting themselves from operations in line with the global war on terrorism to operations in line with great power competition. For example, the US Navy's Daily News Service included a large section titled "Great Power Competition." In addition, courses and certificate degree programs are being offered on this. The stimulus for these academic programs came from the US Navy Staff, with fulfillment through various military institutions of higher education to include the Naval War College and the Naval Postgraduate School.[11] On March 17, 2020, the US Navy, Marine Corps, and Coast Guard issued a new maritime strategy identifying China as the biggest long-term threat to the United States.[12] The *Strategic Guidance* of secretary of the Navy, Carlos del Toro, of October 2021, defines China as the most serious challenge facing the US Navy and Marine Corps.[13] The US Air Force has created a think tank, the Office of Commercial and Economic Analysis, to analyze great power competition.[14] The intelligence community has redirected its focus toward China.[15] Further, the theme of great power competition has been picked up by think tanks of all political stripes.

In early October 2022, President Biden published his *National Security Strategy*, which continues the emphasis on great power competition (particularly regarding China), as does the *National Defense Strategy* by Secretary of Defense Lloyd Austin (October 27, 2022).[16]

Despite the term *great power competition*, there is a crucial ambiguity, as the United States and China are so closely integrated economically and technologically. For example, the United States exported $124 billion in goods to China in 2020 and imported $434 billion. This made China the largest supplier of goods to the United States, and China was the third largest consumer of US goods (after Canada and Mexico).[17] One may legitimately ask whether the focus on great power competition and especially on China is real or imagined. A *New York Times* article states: "In Washington, one of the few issues that override partisan divides in Congress is the specter of Chinese competition, in such crucial areas as semiconductors, artificial intelligence and quantum computing."[18] My first response to the question of whether the United States is really engaged in great power competition is simply that I do not know. I no longer have access to classified information that might inform me on the matter. My second response is, at least for the purposes of this book, it doesn't matter. If great power competition is the rationale that defines the roles and missions of the armed forces and elicits funds from Congress to support these roles and missions, the importance of outsourcing security remains the same. What is different is the nature of the things and services that are contracted.[19]

Different Views on Great Power Competition

If one wants confirmation that the competition at the strategic military level with China, and to a lesser extent Russia, is real, there is ample evidence. One only need read *Un-Restricted Warfare* of 1999 or "Is 'Made in China 2025' a Threat to Global Trade?"[20] The former shows how China can militarily defeat the United States. The latter is a national strategic plan to further develop the manufacturing sector to make China dominant in global high-tech manufacturing technologies. The goal is to catch up with, and surpass, Western technological prowess in advanced industries, executed through a whole-of-government approach to include state-sponsored theft of intellectual property. China is infamous for civil-military fusion, which signifies the government has access to all information, including from the private sector, that could prove useful for military purposes.

In our work in civil-military relations, we find support for seeing China as a serious military competitor to the United States. You Ji of the University of Macau in the People's Republic of China makes it very clear that China's military strategy focuses on the United States and seeks to improve its capability through the adoption of the latest military technologies. The most relevant critical point for me in You Ji's work is the following: "For CCP leaders, a world-class [People's Liberation Army] is a guarantee for China's political system to survive and a source of its legitimacy to rule in the context of safeguarding the country against external threats."[21] That is, the power of the supreme leader, Xi Jinping, is closely tied to the effectiveness of the military. Thus, in China the power of the supreme leaders is intricately linked to military prowess, largely in contrast to the United States.

A recent Congressional Research Service report, "Emerging Military Technologies: Background and Issues for Congress," reviews six emerging military technologies, and for five of them—artificial intelligence, quantum technology, hypersonic weapons, biotechnology, and directed-energy weapons—the report finds that China has made major strides to catch up to the United States.[22]

On the other hand, if one doubts the threat of China to US national security, there is a respectable literature. I will not go into detail on it here beyond acknowledging that it exists. For me in this book what is important is what is accepted politically by the US Congress, DoD, and the armed services, and how the strategy defined in the 2018 national defense strategy is implemented in terms of emerging military technologies and contracting out to obtain them.[23]

Focus on Cyber and Emerging Technologies

This book is about DoD outsourcing, which today concerns advanced or emerging technology for military purpose. Therefore, while there is no doubt that the Chinese state, as well as other states, nonstate actors, terrorist organizations, and common criminals, are involved in conducting cyber attacks on the United States, and other countries, seeking to influence elections, steal intellectual property and technology, and engage in other malign activities, the focus here cannot be exclusively on cyber. Admittedly, DoD has responded in many ways to cyber challenges, including the creation of Cyber Command in 2010.[24] In the huge literature, of particular importance regarding the topic of this book is the work of the Cyberspace Solarium Commission, which deals with virtually all aspects of US national security and cyber.[25] Of those that concern cyber and outsourcing, undoubtedly the greatest current issue is cyber security, mainly of contractors, which is most recently manifested in the 2020 Cybersecurity Maturity Model Certification (CMMC), which is intended to improve the cyber security of contractors.[26] While obviously very necessary, the CMMC poses a challenge for smaller contracting firms, including startups, due to the "sunk costs" of achieving the certification. According to one apparently reliable source: "[Out]sourcing an assessment comes with an estimated cost of $15,000–$45,000, and investments to reach requisite certification levels range from $3,000–$100,000."[27]

Cyber, regardless of how broadly the issues involved are defined, is but one of the "emerging technologies" for those responsible for implementing the 2018 national defense strategy. A recent CRS report lists six "emerging technologies" that could have "a disruptive impact on U.S. national security in the years to come." Cyber is not listed; the "emerging technologies" are artificial intelligence, lethal autonomous weapons, hypersonic weapons, directed-energy weapons, biotechnology, and quantum technology.[28]

Implications for Acquisition in Great Power Competition

In order to lead into the focus in the rest of this chapter and Chapter 6, I will draw on a report by the Government Accountability Office. "Military Acquisitions: DOD Is Taking Steps to Address Challenges Faced by Certain Companies" was prepared in response to a request by the Senate Committee on Armed Services, chaired by the late Senator John McCain. In the cover letter to Senators McCain and Reed, the report states:

> In 1987, DOD accounted for about 40 percent of all research and development spending in the United States. However, the focus and pace of research and development changed dramatically over the decades. By 2013, DOD accounted for less than 20 percent of the spending. Innovation is now being driven by the commercial sector. The commercial sector increased its research and development spending almost 200 percent from 1987 to 2013. Companies are developing sophisticated data analytics software packages, advanced cybersecurity capabilities, and autonomous vehicles that could be used by DOD.[29]

The point raised in this quote makes it clear why DoD has to go to the private, or commercial, sector to obtain the "emerging technology" in order to compete in the challenges posed in the 2018 national defense strategy.

This tremendously important issue is well summarized in a report by one of the most highly regarded experts on technological innovation published by what the report refers to as "the world's leading science and technology think tank" in the following terms:

> In the post-war period, the United States developed the world's most effective national innovation system.... Through a set of

policies, and most importantly, vast government investment in R & D, most of it focused on maintaining a technological and military advantage over the Soviet Union, the United States became the clear leader in technology. But the fall of the Soviet Union meant that policymakers no longer felt an urgency and presided over the gradual and inexorable shrinking of this once preeminent system. . . . As such, the U.S. national innovation system today is in crisis, and in need of thorough rejuvenation, especially through significant increases in federal government funding. Fortunately, as reflected by the growing realization of the China technology challenge and the resultant recent bipartisan congressional advanced technology legislation, there is a growing awareness of this need.[30]

There is a huge amount of documentation—data, analysis, and position papers—on the general issue of innovation in support of emerging technologies, several of which have military relevance. There is no doubt as to the relevance of the issue. It is highlighted in the book by Secretary of Defense Ash Carter and in reports by the CRS and a wide spectrum of think tanks.[31] In addition to the challenges involved in outsourcing discussed in this chapter and the next, there is a major consideration of the current response of the United States on this issue. The enacted NDAA for fiscal year 2022 (S. 1605; Public Law 117-81) authorized $117.7 billion for research, development, test, and evaluation, which was 5.1 percent more than the president's request.[32] While very important, for the foreseeable future technological developments, including in the area of emerging military technologies, will be largely within the private sector. It is in this regard that the issue of defense acquisition—outsourcing—is crucial.

In the December 3, 2020, CRS report "Renewed Great Power Competition," the issue was stated as follows:

> DOD officials and other observers argue that to facilitate greater innovation and speed in weapon system development and deployment, the U.S. defense acquisition policy and the oversight paradigm for assessing the success of acquisition programs will need to be adjusted to place a greater emphasis on innovation and speed as measures of merit in defense acquisition policy, alongside more traditional measures of merit such as minimizing cost growth, schedule delays, and problems in testing."[33]

The awareness that a quicker acquisition mechanism is needed anticipates the focus in the 2018 national defense strategy. Already, in July 2009, the Defense Science Board published a report, "Fulfillment of Urgent Operational Needs," of which the extremely respected and late Jacques Gansler was chairman, that recommended other mechanisms to fulfilling urgent needs in DoD.[34]

A GAO report in 2017 analyzed six challenges facing nontraditional, innovative companies providing their products and services to DoD. Based on GAO interviews with twelve nontraditional companies: "DOD's acquisition environment presents unique challenges to non-traditional companies that they otherwise do not experience in the private industry. The acquisition environment is driven by laws that provide transparency and fairness, regulations that promote specific socio-economic goals, and DOD's approach for implementing those laws and regulations."[35] There is, in short, awareness of a DoD approach to contracting-out, which seeks to fulfill a series of goals accrued during a very long period of time that, as the just-cited GAO report states, "presents unique challenges to non-traditional companies that they otherwise do not experience in the private industry."[36]

Standard Operating Procedures Don't Work

When I began the research project that resulted in this book, I assumed that DoD could utilize standard outsourcing mechanisms, compliant with the FAR, and award contracts to larger firms such as Booz Allen or SAIC, which would then serve as the "prime" contractor to subcontract to smaller firms, including startups, to acquire the latest technology through an existing mechanism.[37] I asked some of my reliable contacts who work in the world of contracting-out if indeed this was the most common approach, and they emphatically argued that this was not how things worked today. What follows are paraphrased comments from two of them, first from an official of a large "prime" contractor located in Northern Virginia and second from the founder and chief executive officer of a startup, or a potential subcontractor, in Silicon Valley. The prime contractor stated: "You asked if we (or GD [General Dynamics], Raytheon, Harris [L3 Harris], etc.) can deliver the [Defense Innovation Unit] type technologies. I would say yes, but the big integrators have a tendency to swallow up the small companies. They are not friendly prime contractors." And the founder of the Silicon Valley startup stated that working with established firms in the industry "is not in the best interest of the startup. The primes cannot be trusted. And this is common knowledge among the startups. The primes may use the startup as a shiny coin to get the contract. Then, they renegotiate or totally exclude the startup. Thus, the latter, knowing how things work, require DoD to come straight to them." Based on my experience, both academic and professional, with prime contractors, this situation rings true. As the popular aphorisms say: It really is all about money, and the startup business model is not focused on winning government contracts to survive. The awareness that this is a problem is made clear in a July 17, 2020, CRS report that states: "The commercial companies that are often at the forefront of innovation in emerging technologies may be reluctant to partner with DOD due to the complexity of the defense acquisition process."[38] In short, the prevailing opinion is that if DoD wants to have access to the latest technological developments, there is no alternative but to deal directly with the startups, and in their environment or ecosystem.[39]

Is the FAR an Impediment to Acquiring Emerging Technology?

In Chapter 4, on outsourcing of intelligence, I discussed the initiative of the Central Intelligence Agency in founding In-Q-Tel in Silicon Valley. As Jon D. Michaels states in his *Virginia Law Review* article: A "private non-profit organization, In-Q-Tel is entrusted to be the Intelligence Community's gateway to the future, investing in and incubating new technologies that will give our spies a leg up on the bad guys for years to come."[40] The problem is that while much of what DoD does is classified, it does not have the freedom, or liberty, of the CIA in terms of acquisitions. As Michaels states: "The CIA can establish shady front operations, procure goods and services unburdened by the onerous Federal Acquisition Regulation . . . and enter into secret personnel contracts that are unenforceable in court."[41] The strategy of In-Q-Tel in identifying, encouraging, and acquiring new technologies, therefore, is not open to the DoD, which must follow rules and regulations from which the intelligence community is exempt, unlike with the CIA, for which, as Michaels states, "most everything that the spy agency does is largely free from legal control." He further states: "Federal agencies subject to the FAR must comply with a host of regulatory constraints. Dutiful adherence limits those agencies' discretion and flexibility, slowing down the process by which they enter contracts for services and goods. Moreover, the procedural hassles that go together with FAR compliance might well deter private firms from pursuing business opportunities with government agencies."[42]

Why and How Is the FAR an Impediment to Obtaining New Technologies?

In Chapter 2, I quoted Scott A. Stanberry to the effect that the FAR is the bible for anyone seeking to win contracts from the US government. Rather than a bible, for me the analogy appears to be that those who specialize in it are comparable to scholars studying the Talmud, as well as the Torah and Halacha, in finding just the precise section in the texts to allow, or prohibit, some action. Considering the length and complexity of the FAR, it is daunting to have to deal with it. I have found the summary in a master of business administration thesis by two military contracting officers in the acquisition management curriculum at the Naval Postgraduate School to be very succinct and useful. After defining the acquisition process, which is the basis for contracting-out in accord with the FAR, they conclude: "In following the traditional procurement policy in an effort to mitigate risk, the defense acquisition community largely disregards the accompanying costs of traditional acquisition methods. This compliance-centered approach offers little flexibility but provides a sense of process security and integrity to the acquisition community and oversight bodies."[43] From all that I can gather by reading and interviews, in the periodic efforts to speed up, adapt, and modernize acquisitions, in order to outsource more quickly, the FAR remains the basis. In the words of probably the most active and vocal proponent of the use of Other Transaction Authorities, Richard L. Dunn, in calling attention to the numerous partial alternatives to the formal (FAR-based) acquisition system, writes: "The mere existence of so many alternative programs is evidence that the traditional system is not deemed to be either rapid or agile, or, to meet critical needs of troops in combat."[44]

To make a transition between the FAR and the main topic of the next chapter, OTAs, I now quote the eloquent statement by a proponent of the OTA as an alternative legal framework for DoD to obtain technical innovations rapidly:

> I have found that the DoD acquisition system is designed primarily for FAR-type actions and has evolved this way in the spirit of doing right with taxpayer money, vetting patriotic vendors, and trying our best to implement technologies that not only serve their functions but also are maintainable/sustainable through our military systems (logistics, maintenance, interoperability with existing systems, etc.). I believe that until recent decades, this has served us well because we had such technological superiority, there was no real threat to being too slow to adopt. However, an advanced industrial base both at home and abroad that is way faster, more agile, and creative in how it employs threats has created an edge in that we cannot react, let alone stay ahead, of these methods (I'm thinking cyber, information, and space capabilities primarily). Adapting to these threats does not jive well with the FAR way of doing things (unfortunately).[45]

Conclusion

The 2018 national defense strategy is a real strategy. The strategy, in line with initiatives already in place during the administration of President Barack Obama, posits the need to compete with China. Research and development of newer defense technology, however, lagged at the end of the Cold War, continuing to do so in the intervening two decades and during the global war on terrorism, and other countries made major advances in research and development with military applications. There is general agreement that DoD, and the armed services, must quickly accelerate research and development in these areas, and this requires outsourcing. Unofficial and official documents, including those of CRS and GAO, highlight, however, that the acquisition system, based upon the FAR, currently utilized by DoD, is unable to quickly adapt to these emergent needs. Rather than a particular failure in acquisitions, the constraints involved in working with the FAR are better understood in terms of opportunity costs. While the traditional defense contracting firms are geared up to deal with the FAR, other, nontraditional firms, and especially startups, in the words of experts on outsourcing, "don't want to work with DoD."

Notes

1. While most authors begin with Carl von Clausewitz, major contemporary contributions to this literature have been made by John Lewis Gaddis, *On Grand Strategy* (New York: Penguin, 2019), whom I draw upon in Chapter 1 of this book; and Hew Strachan, *The Direction of War: Contemporary Strategy in Historical Perspective* (Cambridge: Cambridge University Press, 2013). One of the major contributions of Strachan's book, and articles, is his focus on civil-military relations in the development of strategy.

2. I have utilized this framework to analyze national defense strategies in Chile, Colombia, Portugal, and the United States. See my "Requirements for Military Effectiveness: Chile in Comparative Perspective" (Washington, DC: William J. Perry Center for Hemispheric Defense Studies, March 2020); and my "Effectiveness in Comparative Perspective," in Carlos Solar, ed., *The Armed Forces and Democracy: Governing the Military in Chile* (Manchester: Manchester University Press, forthcoming 2022).

3. Kathleen H. Hicks and Andrew Hunter, "Assessing the Third Offset Strategy" (Washington, DC: Center for Strategic and International Studies, March 2017), p. 1.

4. World Bank data available at https://data.worldbank.org/indicator/MS.MIL.XPND.CD.

5. The most recent in my possession is Ronald O'Rourke, "Renewed Great Power Competition: Implications for Defense—Issues for Congress" (Washington, DC: Congressional Research Service, December 21, 2021). The Federation of American Scientists website hosting these reports indicates that its predecessor was the seventy-ninth version: https://crsreports.congress.gov/product/details?prodcode=R43838.

6. No author, February 5, 2018.

7. *Providing for the Common Defense: The Assessment and Recommendations of the National Defense Strategy Commission,* 2019, https://www.hsdl.org/c/sign-in/?dest=abstract%26did%3D818823.

8. *CRS In Focus,* "Evaluating DOD Strategy: Key Findings of the National Defense Strategy Commission" (Washington, DC: Congressional Research Service, March 19, 2019).

9. National Defense Authorization Act for 2020, which became Public Law 116-92 on December 20, 2019; https://www.congress.gov/bill/116th-congress/senate-bill/1790, p. 133.

10. James O. Ellis, James N. Mattis, and Kori Schake, "Restoring Our National Security," in George P. Shultz, ed., *Blueprint for America* (Stanford: Hoover Institution, 2016), pp. 137–150.

11. See, for example, https://www.navy.mil/Press-Office/News-Stories/display-news/Article/2351609/nps-launches-distance-learning-graduate-certificate-in-great-power-competition.

12. See https://www.military.com/daily-news/2020/12/17/new-naval-strategy-zeroes-china-biggest-long-term-threat-us.html.

13. See the headline on China, for example, at https://www.defensedaily.com/secnav-releases-strategic-guidance-focusing-on-china/navy-usmc.

14. See https://www.afocea.com.

15. Julian A. Barnes, "C.I.A. Chief Is Reorganizing Agency to Focus on Challenges from China," *New York Times,* October 2, 2021, p. A10.

16. President Joe Biden, *National Security Strategy* (Washington, DC: The White House, October 2022); US Department of Defense, *2022 National Defense Strategy* (Washington, DC: Secretary of Defense, October 27, 2022).

17. David E. Sanger, "Don't Call It a Cold War: U.S. Labors to Name China Rivalry," *New York Times,* October 18, 2021, pp. 1, A5.

18. Ibid.

19. For insights into the nature of the adversary, from the perspective of DoD, it is worth reviewing a recent report from DoD on China: https://media.defense.gov/2020/Sep/01/2002488689/-1/-1/1/2020-dod-china-military-power-report-final.pdf.

20. See Quao Liang and Wang Xiangsui, *Un-Restricted Warfare* (Brattleboro, VT: Echo Point Books and Media, 1999); James McBride and Andrew Chatzky, "Is 'Made in China 2025' a Threat to Global Trade?" (Washington, DC: Council on Foreign Relations, May 13, 2019), https://www.cfr.org/backgrounder/made-china-2025-threat-global-trade.

21. You Ji, "China: Traditions, Institutions, and Effectiveness," in Thomas C. Bruneau and Aurel Croissant, eds., *Civil-Military Relations: Control and Effectiveness Across Regimes* (Boulder: Lynne Rienner, 2019), p. 218.

22. Kelley M. Sayler, "Emerging Military Technologies: Background and Issues for Congress" (Washington, DC: Congressional Research Service, November 10, 2021). There is a huge literature, including US government–sponsored reports, on virtually all these emerging technologies. See, for example, on quantum technology, Defense Science Board, *Applications of Quantum Technologies: Executive Summary* (Washington, DC: Office of the

Undersecretary of Defense for Research and Engineering, October 2019), https://dsb.cto.mil/reports.htm; and for an article in the major science journal, *Scientific American*, see https://www.scientificamerican.com/article/china-reaches-new-milestone-in-space-based-quantum-communications. A relevant perspective for this book is found in Department of Defense, Office of the Secretary of Defense, *Military and Security Developments Involving the People's Republic of China 2021 Annual Report to Congress*. This report is done in accord with Section 1202 of the NDAA of fiscal year 2020.

23. Much of the literature is included within the field of security studies in the subdiscipline of international relations. For an excellent example, see Andrea Gilli and Mauro Gilli, "Why China Has Not Caught Up Yet," *International Security* 43, no. 3 (Winter 2018), pp. 141–189, as well as the debate on this issue continued in the same journal, 44, no. 2 (Fall 2019), pp. 185–92. See also Evan S. Medeiros and Jude Blanchette, "Beyond Colossus or Collapse: Five Myths Driving American Debates About China," *War on the Rocks*, March 19, 2021. Thomas J. Christensen of Columbia University writes and speaks extensively on this topic from a professional and academic perspective. See his book *The China Challenge: Shaping the Choices of a Rising Power* (New York: Norton, 2015).

24. A useful review of Cyber Command and its activities is Paul M. Nakasone and Michael Sulmeyer, "How to Compete in Cyberspace: Cyber Command's New Approach," *Foreign Affairs* (September–October 2020), https://www.foreignaffairs.com/articles/united-states/2020-08-25/cybersecurity.

25. For the report of the Cyberspace Solarium Commission, see https://www.solarium.gov/report. See also, for example, Catherine A. Theohary and John W. Rollins, "Cyberwarfare and Cyberterrorism: In Brief" (Washington, DC: Congressional Research Service, March 27, 2015); and to get an idea of the concern by the US Congress regarding cyber issues, see GAO, "Report to Congressional Requesters: Cybersecurity: Clarity of Leadership Urgently Needed to Fully Implement the National Strategy" (Washington, DC, September 2020). See also Department of Defense Science Board, "Task Force on Cyber Deterrence" (Washington, DC: Office of the Undersecretary of Defense for Acquisition, Technology, and Logistics, February 2017), https://dsb.cto.mil/reports/2010s/DSB-CyberDeterrenceReport_02-28-17_Final.pdf.

26. My statement on the importance of cybersecurity to DoD and its use of contractors is based on the attention given by Congress as demonstrated by numerous GAO reports, and to DoD by its publications. See, for example, GAO, "Report to Congressional Committees: Cybersecurity: DOD Needs to Take Decisive Actions to Improve Cyber Hygiene" (Washington, DC, April 2020). On the CMMC, see, for example, https://www.acq.osd.mil/cmmc; and Heidi M. Peters, "Defense Acquisitions: DOD's

Cybersecurity Maturity Model Certification Framework" (Washington, DC: Congressional Research Service, December 18, 2020). There is now an emerging industry whose role it is to bring contracting firms up to CMMC standards. For an authoritative and skeptical view of the CMMC, see Frank Kendall, "Cybersecurity Maturity Model Certification: An Idea Whose Time Has Not Come and Never May," *Forbes*, April 29, 2020, https://www.forbes.com/sites/frankkendall/2020/04/29/cyber-security-maturity-model-certificationan-idea-whose-time-has-not-come-and-never-may/?sh=7df25d73bf2d.

27. Amanda Bresler and Alex Bresler, "Analyzing the Composition of the Department of Defense Small Business Industrial Base," 2021, https://media-exp1.licdn.com/dms/document/C4D1FAQEOxhFMS9MKRg/feedshare-document-pdf-analyzed/0/1650309424054?e=2147483647&v=beta&t=nryjkSKhaiXj-VvGUXgZhnFSCT4XonrsZ6QHHJyHT4c. This excellent paper by the Breslers deals with the issue of decreasing competition in the so-called defense industrial base. See US Department of Defense, "State of Competition Within the Defense Industrial Base" (Washington, DC, February 2022).

28. *CRS In Focus*, "Defense Primer: Emerging Technologies" (Washington, DC, June 8, 2021). There is also the previously noted report by Sayler, "Emerging Military Technologies."

29. GAO, "Military Acquisitions: DOD Is Taking Steps to Address Challenges Faced by Certain Companies" (Washington, DC, July 2017), p. 1.

30. Robert D. Atkinson, "Understanding the U.S. National Innovation System, 2020" (Washington, DC: Information Technology and Innovation Foundation, November 2020), p. 1. For an earlier quote on its importance, see p. 25. For an effort to evaluate the readiness, which is done by mandate in the NDAA for fiscal year 2019, see GAO, "Military Readiness: Department of Defense Domain Readiness Varied from Fiscal Year 2017 Through Fiscal Year 2019" (Washington, DC, April 2021). The results are concerning, as the report notes that sea domain readiness decreased while space and cyber were mixed. As the focus today is China, which involves the sea, space, and cyber, there are serious implications following from the study.

31. Ash Carter, *Inside the Five-Sided Box: Lessons from a Lifetime of Leadership in the Pentagon* (New York: Dutton, 2019), states: "Technological superiority is an absolute necessity if the U.S. military is to be successful in carrying out its missions around the world" (p. 329). For further information on this issue, see: John F. Sargent Jr., "The Global Research and Development Landscape and Implications for the Department of Defense" (Washington, DC: Congressional Research Service, June 28, 2021); James Andrew Lewis, "National Security and the Innovation Ecosystem" (Washington, DC: CSIS, October 2021); and "America's

Eroding Technological Advantage: National Defense Strategy RT&E Priorities in an Era of Great-Power Competition with China" (Arlington, VA: Govini, 2020).

32. *CRS Insight,* "FY 2022 NDAA: Research, Development, Test, and Evaluation Authorizations" (Washington, DC, March 18, 2022).

33. Ronald O'Rourke, "Renewed Great Power Competition: Implications for Defense—Issues for Congress" (Washington, DC: Congressional Research Service, December 2, 2021), pp. 17–18. *The Future of Defense Task Force Report 2020* makes essentially the same points regarding reforms to the acquisition process; see pp. 67–69, https://armedservices.house.gov/_cache/files/2/6/26129500-d208-47ba-a9f7-25a8f82828b0/6D5C75605DE8DDF0013712923B4388D7.future-of-defense-task-force-report.pdf.

34. Office of the Undersecretary of Defense for Acquisition, Technology, and Logistics, *Report of the Defense Science Board Task Force on Fulfillment of Urgent Operational Needs* (Washington, DC, July 2009), https://dsb.cto.mil/reports/2000s/ADA503382.pdf.

35. GAO, "Military Acquisitions" (Washington, DC, July 2017), p. 8

36. Ibid.

37. This is indeed the impression one would get by reading *Defense News,* a trade publication of the industry, on July 13, 2022. The title is "Booz Allen Unveils $100 M Venture Capital Fund to Back Tech Startups," https://www.defensenews.com/industry/2022/07/13/booz-allen-unveils-100m-venture-capital-fund-to-back-tech-startups/. But one of these "startups" turned out to be AEye. AEye was founded in 2013 and is a publicly traded company. It is clearly not a startup, but a very well established and recognized company.

38. Sayler, "Emerging Military Technologies."

39. On this issue, see, for example, Rachel Olney, "The Rift Between Silicon Valley and the Pentagon Is Economic, Not Moral," *War on the Rocks,* January 28, 2018. For a less "economic" interpretation, see, for example, Amy Zegart and Kevin Childs, "The Divide Between Silicon Valley and Washington Is a National Security Threat," *The Atlantic,* December 13, 2018.

40. Jon D. Michaels, "The (Willingly) Fettered Executive: Presidential Spinoffs in National Security Domains and Beyond," *Virginia Law Review* 97, no. 4 (May 19, 2011), p. 805.

41. Ibid., p. 806. Maybe stated more accurately, DoD has not, and quite possibly cannot, take advantage of a national security exception to full and open competition stipulated in the FAR. On this point, see GAO, "Defense Contracting: Improved Policies and Tools Could Help Increase Competition on DOD's National Security Exception Procurements" (Washington, DC, January 2012).

42. Michaels, "The (Willingly) Fettered Executive," p. 835.

43. Jacob D. Sabin and Mark K. Zakner, "Analysis of Expedited Defense Contracting Methods in the Acquisition of Emerging Technology" (Monterey, CA: Naval Postgraduate School, December 2016), p. 11.

44. Richard L. Dunn, "Injecting New Ideas and New Approaches in Defense Systems: Are 'Other Transactions' an Answer?" May 2009, p. 2, https://nps.edu/web/acqnresearch/dair.

45. Written comment from a staff member of the Naval Postgraduate School's Emerging Technology Consortium to Thomas Bruneau, July 3, 2020. The consortium utilizes non-FAR mechanisms in developing "innovation hubs" in which NPS would, as a research lab, partner in a consortium with high-tech industry to import innovations into DoD.

6

Developing Advanced Technologies

THE JULY 2017 GAO REPORT, REQUESTED BY SENATORS MCCAIN AND Reed, cited in Chapter 5, calls specific attention to provision of Other Transaction Authority by Congress and to the role of the Defense Innovation Unit (DIU) in utilizing OTAs to enter into agreements with industry for prototyping agreements.[1] This sense or spirit of the GAO report conveys an awareness of the perceived need for newer technologies with a legal framework that is less ponderous than the traditional, FAR-based framework.

Defense Innovation Unit and Silicon Valley

I reported in Chapter 4 that the intelligence community created In-Q-Tel to obtain the most innovative technology in cyber. In-Q-Tel is not bound by the terms of the FAR due to a national security waiver. Secretary of Defense Ash Carter created the DIU in 2015 "to help build bridges between the Pentagon and commercial technology firms, including startups."[2] What is most important here about the innovations of the DIU is that they utilize OTAs in their innovative work, first in Silicon Valley, and later in Austin, Boston, the Pentagon, and most recently Chicago. As the website of DIU states: "DIU connects its DoD partners with leading technology companies across the country."[3]

The most common reference in the development of advanced technology is Silicon Valley. The IC established In-Q-Tel first in Silicon

Valley in 1999, and Secretary of Defense Carter established DIU there in 2015. The NDAA for fiscal year 2016 specifically refers to Silicon Valley in relationship to the use of OTAs: "The conferees believe that expanded use of OTAs will support Department of Defense efforts to access new sources of technical innovation, such as Silicon Valley startup companies and small commercial firms."[4] *The Economist* of November 21, 2020, states: "Silicon Valley is more visited by foreign dignitaries and finders-of-fact than any other business locale in the world. One of its tech giants is currently worth $21trn; three more are worth more than $11.1trn. The contribution technology makes to the buoyancy of its markets is without equal."[5] Silicon Valley is the hub of the newest technologies in the world. According to Stanford University professor and expert on intelligence and national security Amy Zegart, this is due to four main factors that together are not duplicated anywhere else in the world. They are the proximity of two major research universities—Stanford University and the University of California at Berkeley; location on the West Coast and consequently a large degree of independence from government based in Washington, DC; a free and active capital market characterized by the predominance of venture capital; and adherence to the rule of law.[6] Despite numerous attempts throughout the United States and indeed the world, this ecosystem of technological breakthroughs, characterized by not only the giants of Google and Facebook, but also a huge number of startups, has never been duplicated.

In the context of this book and specifically the authorities to acquire innovative technologies, I believe it is worth elaborating on Zegart's four factors. Based on my experience at Berkeley and Stanford, as well as from visiting universities throughout the United States, Western Europe, and elsewhere, I agree with Zegart.[7] The quality of education and research at these two nearby universities is unparalleled in the world. Second, the distance from Washington, DC, is positive in the sense that there is no political "truth" in Silicon Valley, and the West Coast in general; and one can largely ignore the political antics taking place in Washington, DC, and the commentaries on them. Third, venture capital is huge; for example, Theranos raised $700 million largely in venture capital and reached a valuation of $10 billion before it folded. Fourth, the rule of law is taken for granted in the United States, including Silicon Valley, but is not in Brazil, China, India, Russia, and others.

Based on my familiarity with Silicon Valley and the specific research for this book, I believe the reference to Silicon Valley regarding acquisition authorities is largely symbolic. Indeed, it is a major source for innovations, and the DIU, which has oversight over the National Security Innovation Capital (NSIC) and the National Security Innovation Network (NSIN), appears to be extremely successful in identifying and acquiring new technologies.[8] However, too great a focus on Silicon Valley in terms of acquisition of defense-related new technologies is misleading. The Silicon Valley ecosystem is defined by two main features. First is the dynamic of venture capital, which rewards abundantly and punishes without compassion.[9] Second, it is dominated by individuals who have little if any interest in security, national or otherwise, and are as likely to be from China or India as from the United States. From my perspective, Rachel Olney, who teaches the course "Technology and National Security" at Stanford University and is the chief executive officer of a startup, has it right in her short article in *War on the Rocks* that there are several severe impediments for startups to working with the DoD.[10]

Background and Content of OTAs

While OTAs are typically defined in terms of what they are not, I attempt to provide later in this chapter some of the main elements of what they are and I will use case studies to highlight some of the main points. First, however, what they are not is conveyed in the following quote from William Weinig: "In comparison to the 4,775 pages of policy regulation, and best practices used by most defense acquisition offices, those utilizing OTs for prototype projects are constrained by approximately 65 pages of documentation."[11]

In response to *Sputnik*, the US Congress passed the National Aeronautics and Space Act in July 1958 (Space Act, Public Law 85-568), which established the National Aeronautics and Space Administration (NASA). "In an effort to give the new agency 'the necessary freedom to carry on research, development, and exploration . . . to ensure the full development of these peaceful and defense uses without unnecessary delays,' the Space Act granted NASA broad authority to 'enter into and perform such contracts, leases, cooperative agreement, or *other transactions* as may be necessary' to accomplish its mission of research and exploration."[12] Later, Congress extended different variations of OTAs to specific other agencies, granting the authority to DoD in the fiscal year 1990 and 1991 NDAAs.

In what follows I will summarize and paraphrase the main features of OTAs drawn from several different sources of information.[13] OTAs are legally binding instruments that may be used to engage industry and academia for a broad range of research and prototyping activities. They may include various funding arrangements or may be non-reimbursable, where each party bears the costs of their participation and funds are not exchanged. The length of an OTA is negotiable, ranging from days to years. Under an OTA, intellectual property rights for solutions may be negotiable. In DoD authorities for OTAs there are three types. One, research, is based on 10 US Code 2371 and is intended for basic, applied, and advanced research projects. Two, protype, is authorized under 10 US Code 2371b and is intended for DoD to acquire protype capabilities to transition into production OTAs. And third, a production OTA is authorized under 10 US Code 2373 and is a noncompetitive, follow-on OTA to a prototype other-transaction agreement that was competitively awarded and successfully completed. The last noted—a production OTA—is extremely important. As Stan Soloway, Jason Knudson, and Vincent Wroble state:

> Historically, OTA usage focused solely on research and development. Upon completion of a successful OTA protype, a contract for full production then reverted to traditional FAR coverage. But, the FY 2016 defense authorization bill authorized the use of OTA terms and conditions for the life of a program, recognizing the growing and counterproductive gap in technical capabilities between the government and the commercial sectors.[14]

In addition to the importance assigned by Soloway et al., the amendment (with 10 US Code 2373 resulting in the ability to transition to full production) is an additional positive element of using

10 US Code 2373. As Heidi M. Peters writes: "The term *prototype* is not defined in statute. DOD generally describes a prototype as a physical, virtual, or theoretical model used to evaluate the technical or manufacturing feasibility, or *effectiveness*, of what is intended to come later. It need not be a physical model; prototypes can involve designs, novel applications of commercial technologies, demonstrations of operational utility, and proofs of concept."[15] That is, a protype can be a service as well as a thing. This is relevant since virtually any new technology includes something that could be defined as a service. It is, therefore, not surprising that the title of a recent GAO report is "Defense Acquisitions: DOD's Use of Other Transactions for Prototype Projects Has Increased."[16] If one wants more detail on protypes, a RAND team, led by Lauren A. Mayer, conducted a very thorough study resulting in several recommendations that are consistent with the conclusions of this book.[17]

There are two crucial observations on OTAs. The first is the tremendous flexibility in their use. The second, discussed in the report by Stan Soloway and others, based on extensive empirical research including interviews, is that OTAs meet the main tenets of public procurement, which are competition, transparency and accountability, intellectual property and the protection of the government's rights, disputes and protests, and socioeconomic preferences and diversity.[18]

Even before dealing with the use of OTAs in the Covid pandemic, there were positive assessments by the most relevant government entities—Congress and DoD—of the potential use of OTAs. First, from a CRS report for Congress by Heidi M. Peters: "OTAs have the potential to provide significant benefits to DOD including attracting nontraditional contractors with promising technological capabilities to work with DOD, establishing a mechanism to pool resources with other entities to facilitate development of, and obtain, state-of-the-art dual-use technologies, and offering a unique mechanism for DOD to invest in, and influence the direction of, technology development."[19] Second, from the DoD guide to the use of OTAs: "The [other-transaction] authorities were created to give DoD the flexibility necessary to adopt and incorporate business practices that reflect commercial industry standards and best practices into its award instruments. When leveraged appropriately, [other transactions] provide the Government with access to state-of-the-art technology solutions from traditional and non-traditional defense contractors."[20]

Covid-19 and OTAs

The topic of Covid-19 and the use of OTAs will lead directly into further information on the use of OTAs and their promotion by Congress, in terms of the framework for analysis in this book. There are three excellent reports on this topic, two GAO and one CRS, that provide extensive updated information.[21]

According to the GAO, US government–wide contract obligations in response to the Covid-19 pandemic totaled $17.8 billion as of June 2020.[22] In addition, a more recent GAO report shows that as of March 2021, DoD alone obligated a total of $10.9 billion via OTAs, $7.2 billion of which was via consortia.[23] Of particular importance in the earlier, July 2020, GAO report is the section "Agencies Have a Variety of Contracting Flexibilities to Facilitate Government Response to the COVID-19 Pandemic." The report states: "Agencies can use several existing contracting techniques—based on provisions in the CARES Act and emergency procurement authorities in the FAR—that provide flexibilities to quickly and efficiently award contracts in response to the pandemic."[24] Of the three vehicles listed—Undefinitized Contract Actions, Other Transaction Authority, and Special Emergency Procurement Authorities—only OTAs could inherently, as the GAO report states, "enable federal agencies to negotiate terms and conditions specific to a project without requiring them to comply with certain federal regulations."[25] Whereas the flexibilities extended in the two FAR-based mechanisms necessitated the declaration of a national emergency, in the case of OTAs the modification only concerned approvals for higher cost thresholds and relaxed notification requirements to congressional committees. That is, OTAs could be utilized with relatively minor adjustments in the face of emergency demands.

The July 2021 GAO report paints an extremely positive view of the use of OTAs in the context of the national emergency of the Covid-19 pandemic. The report lists the following positive factors associated with the use of OTAs: timeliness of awards, more flexible contracting process and less administrative work, and nontraditional contractor engagement, with OTAs allowing for cost-sharing and ability to use additional funding streams.[26] In addition, it should be noted that Defense Advanced Research Projects Agency (DARPA), which uses OTAs, played an important role in funding the scientific breakthroughs critical to developing antibody technology used in the Covid-19 vaccine.[27]

The July 2021 GAO report brings up a topic that somewhat relativizes the importance of Silicon Valley in the utilization of OTAs in DoD acquisitions. The report provides details in the use of consortia, and especially "consortia management firms."[28] The emergence of consortia is, as they say, a work in progress. According to Stan Soloway, there are dozens of consortia throughout the United States seeking to partner different parts of DoD and the armed services with high-tech firms, mainly startups, in order to create what the proponents refer to as "innovation hubs," with the goal to build an "ecosystem of innovation."[29] The most recent version of the *NavalX Playbook* in my possession, for instance, lists twenty-three such consortia, and other documents I have reviewed list in excess of thirty.[30] My interviews with members of the Emerging Technology Consortium (ETC) team at the Naval Postgraduate School report that there are between twenty and thirty consortia management firms operating in the United States. Their importance, as made clear in GAO "Covid-19 Contracting: Actions Needed," is the speed and outreach bringing together a large assortment of startup technology firms, research labs, and a variety of government entities. A possible positive outcome of the emergence and growth of these consortia management firms and the ecosystems they spawn is education and experience in the use of OTAs, which currently is not provided through formal education or training.[31]

In the midst of all of the positive implications in the use of OTAs there are, however, two potentially negative factors that particularly emerge from the experience of using OTAs in the Covid-19 pandemic. One is noted in a CRS report on personal protective equipment (PPE) production in the United States. The legal basis for OTAs in 10 US Code 2371(b) does not extend to national health emergencies or other domestic crises.[32] This type of issue, domestic versus foreign defense roles, is extremely important in newer democracies, including Brazil, Indonesia, South Africa, and others.[33] It would be unfortunate if experience in the United States in the face of the national emergency caused by Covid-19 were to provide some degree of legitimacy for the domestic use of the military in countries with less robust institutions than those of the United States for controlling the military.[34]

The second potentially negative factor is highlighted in GAO "Covid-19 Contracting: Actions Needed," which cites extensive evidence in concluding that the tracking of the use of OTAs was problematic, and thus that oversight was questionable. There is no conclusion that any organization was playing loose with US government funds, "the people's money"; rather the conclusion is that there was very low visibility over these funds. This issue leads into the discussion on Congress later in this chapter.

The Intelligence Community and Acquisitions

In Chapter 4, I discussed the IC and acquisition reform in the context of the global war on terrorism. In that chapter I also included reference to In-Q-Tel as a mechanism for the IC to get the latest technology in cyber. Currently, in great power competition, the IC is being strongly encouraged to update in all regards, including acquisition beyond cyber, and at a minimum artificial intelligence. A team at CSIS conducted a major study and produced an important report that embodies the awareness, and details, of this updating. The report is "Maintaining the Intelligence Edge: Reimagining and Reinventing Intelligence Through Innovation." The report includes an important focus on the need to innovate in acquisitions. Although the report itself is unclassified, eleven of the twelve commissioners have all held extremely important positions in the IC, and the twelfth, Amy Zegart, who was on the NSC, is among the most prolific and highly respected academics specializing on intelligence issues. The commission consulted widely, including both the executive branch and the two intelligence oversight committees in Congress. Further, one of the cochairs, Avril Haines, is now the director of national intelligence, and one of two CSIS experts, Kathleen Hicks, is deputy secretary of defense. If there were ever a report by a think tank that is likely to be implemented, this is it. The commission report states: "The dawning era of intelligence innovation must compel the IC to *reimagine* its tradecraft and missions to harness technology potential and *reinvent* its processes, partnerships, workforce, incentives, and— yes—culture to embrace technological transformation."[35]

I believe for the purposes of this book it is worth quoting in full the first paragraph of the executive summary:

> The U.S. Intelligence Community (IC) stands at the dawn of a new era of technological innovation and transformation unprecedented in its history. Driven by artificial intelligence (AI) and associated emerging technologies, including cloud computing and advanced sensors, and big data analytics, the approaching "AI era" will transform both the nature of the global threats the IC is responsible for assessing and the IC's ability to accurately detect and assess them. Through all of this, the core mission of the IC will remain unchanged: to understand what is happening in the world, to deliver timely, accurate, and insightful analysis of those threats and developments to U.S. policymakers, and to provide U.S. leaders decision making advantages over competitors. What will change is the IC's ability to fulfill this mission if it does not adapt to the new AI era.

The report analyzes *enablers* and defines them as those elements that are crucial for "the IC to seize the potential of emerging technologies."[36] The report highlights an acquisition process that rapidly distributes cutting-edge technology to users for adoption and mission integration. In the previous year, 2020, in a report of the House Permanent Select Committee on Intelligence, the issue of acquisitions was identified as a critical handicap for the IC.[37] Under the rubric "Rethink Acquisition Procedures and Culture" the CSIS report recommends that the IC rethink how it purchases goods and services. The House Committee identifies a problem in acquisitions by calling attention to the complicated web of federal acquisition laws and, with reference to the IC, the obligation to possess high-level security clearances. It calls specific attention to OTAs and raises the question of why the IC is (or isn't) leveraging OTAs, and emphatically recommends "that the IC produce a report that examines the use of OTA by IC elements on a yearly basis and provide that report to this Committee."[38]

The CSIS report goes into detail on the need for major improvements in acquisitions. It states: "In short, the U.S. IC cannot compete in the global intelligence arena and fulfill its vital missions without a reinvention of how it procures, adopts, and assimilates emerging technologies and delivers them to mission users—at speed and at scale."[39] Consequently, in the section on *enablers*, the report goes into detail under the following rubrics: "Refresh the IC's Acquisition Tool Kit" and "Integrate IC and DOD Acquisition Strategies."[40] The latter point is extremely important both in terms of utilizing, as is DoD, more flexible acquisition authorities, and in recognizing that while the IC and DoD are not identical, they face similar challenges in acquisitions. Further, and similar to DoD, the report states the following: "The private sector will be the primary source of innovation for many, if not most, of the near-term technologies analyzed in this report."[41] The report makes recommendations that directly concern acquisition reform. I believe it is worth quoting one of these in full: "The IC should prioritize *training of contracting officials on rapid authorities* and new approaches for procurement of software, AI, and associated advanced technologies."[42] The sense of the recommendation is very similar to the mandate in the fiscal year 2018 NDAA, codified in 10 US Code 2371(g), to provide adequate education and training to program managers and technical and contracting personnel in the use of OTAs and other forms of innovative contracting.[43]

Congress

Congress has been tremendously supportive in promoting the use of OTAs in DoD ever since it extended the use of OTAs to DoD in the NDAAs for 1990 and 1991, and in subsequent NDAAs has both continued to support them and encouraged the expansion of their use.[44] The 2016 NDAA authorized the use of OTAs for the life of a program and the 2018 NDAA required the DoD to: "establish a *preference* for using OTs for the execution of science and technology and prototyping programs; and, provide OT education and training to its management, contracting, and program management workforce and to establish OT continuous learning and certification requirements for the workforce."[45] The 2019 and 2020 NDAAs elaborated on and clarified reporting requirements using OTAs. And the NDAA for fiscal year 2021, which was finalized by Congress in early December 2020, extended OTA to additional executive branch components and authorized the use of OT agreements under new circumstances (such as the CARES Act and raising the dollar limit on the use of OTAs). In the NDAA for fiscal year 2022 there is only minor tinkering with OTA policies, but included is a request, in Section 824, for DoD to advise Congress how OTAs could be modified or expanded.

There is an abundance of expanded authorities in the annual NDAAs demonstrating the support of Congress for the use of OTAs. This expansion of authorities has been recognized by various experts on this topic. The research report by Soloway, Knudson, and Wroble has already been cited extensively. In addition, Weinig states the following: "The record shows Congress increasingly believes prototype OTs to be the mechanism capable of bridging the gap between the DoD and industry. Actions supporting this assertion begin in earnest in the 2016 NDAA. This legislation expanded and made permanent the prototype OT authority."[46] Richard Beutel, highly respected expert in government contracting in the industry, summarized for me how the US Congress has encouraged the use of OTA: "OTAs by their initial design were intended to pipeline risky but emerging technologies into government using rapid prototyping and agile development practices to minimize development risk. However, over the last several legislative cycles, they have expanded to include follow-on production contracts, as well as a broader interpretation of what a 'prototype' looks like in terms of using OTA authorities."[47] Beutel's message to me, and the large number of briefings on the use of OTAs by consultants for the "industry," suggest to me that the "industry" "gets it." In the February 22, 2019, CRS report on OTAs, the author raised the possibility that Congress might "clamp down on the authority."[48] This has not happened. However, in the fiscal year 2022 NDAA, consistent with GAO-21-501, Congress requested further information on the use of OTAs.[49] In conclusion, Congress has been and continues until the present to be extremely supportive of the use of OTAs by DoD.

Education and Training

In making virtually no effort in this research to obtain briefs by consultants for the industry on the use of OTAs, I accumulated seven in less than two years. All seven are thoroughly documented and logical, provide useful insights for business, and are well presented with citations. Several are listed in the bibliography of this book. The mandate for education and training for the "agreement officers" was stipulated in the 2018 NDAA for DoD as "provide OT education and training to its management, contracting, and program management workforce and to establish OT continuous learning and certification requirements for the workforce."[50] Also Crane Lopes, in his comprehensive dissertation on OTAs, calls particular attention to the guidance of DoD to, as he puts it, "encourage flexibility and innovation by agreements officers during OT negotiations."[51] Lopes goes into detail in emphasizing the importance of the agreement officer, since so much leeway is given to him or her. As Lopes writes: "Thus, the agreements officer must be experienced and exercise sound business judgment on behalf of the government. For instance, the agreements officer should make sure that the cost to the government is reasonable and that the schedule and other requirements of the project can be met. Experienced agreements officers are critical to the success of [other-transaction] negotiations."[52] In conclusion, however, he finds: "There is insufficient training and policy guidance for [other transactions]. Study participants remarked that the DoD workforce is only trained to use traditional procurement agreements, not [other transactions]."[53] He, like I, found that the Defense Acquisition University offers a few courses, but "it is apparent that many DoD employees lack expertise, even basic knowledge about [other transactions]. Congress has recently taken legislative action in response to this problem."[54] Yet, despite this legislative action, [the mandate in the 2018 NDAA] from my research, and according to the leading proponent of the use of OTAs, Richard Dunn of the Strategic Institute FOR Innovation in Government Contracting, the NDAA section, codified as 10 US Code 2371(g), "has never really been implemented."[55] That is, unless the following qualifies as implementation: "Defense Acquisition University, Administration of

Other Transactions (CLC 102)—web based continuous learning module, approximately 1.5 hours to complete."[56]

The reader may recall the content of the fifth recommendation of the CSIS report in which the current DNI and deputy secretary of defense participated. It reads as follows: "The IC should prioritize *training of contracting officials on rapid authorities* and new approaches for procurement of software, AI, and associated advanced technologies."[57] However, prior to their nominations and confirmations, Michele A. Flournoy, former undersecretary of defense for policy, in her testimony before the House Armed Services Committee on the topic "DOD's Role in the Competition with China," raised an extremely important point: "In the acquisition workforce, DoD has not adequately trained or *incentivized* employees to use the flexible authorities Congress has provided. While there are pockets of excellence (e.g., in SOCOM and Air Force acquisition), the bulk of the acquisition corps is not using these authorities effectively, consistently and at scale."[58]

According to the Federal News Network on November 4, 2021, DoD used OTA agreements for $16.2 billion of contracts in fiscal year 2020. The article said that while data for fiscal year 2021 were not yet available, the sum should be larger.[59] In fiscal year 2020, DoD contracted out $420 billion. Therefore, OTAs constituted less than 4 percent of total contracts, and even if the sum in fiscal year 2021 is larger, one still must ask why OTAs constituted, at the most, 5 percent of all contracts when Congress promotes their use and when all available reports by the CRS, the GAO, and "the industry" are extremely positive. The reference in the preceding paragraph by Flournoy to training and incentives is, in my opinion, crucial. In a podcast from the Center for Government Contracting at George Mason University, both Stan Soloway and Wes Bennett of DARPA brought up again and again the workforce issue. One can speculate whether the lack of training and education is the cause or effect of what is termed a "risk-averse" attitude of contracting officers, but a potential cause is discussed later in this chapter.[60] It should be remembered that the workforce issue was identified as a problem in the Packard Commission report in 1986, as noted in Chapter 1.

Case Studies of the Use of Other Transaction Authorities

In this section I will provide two case studies of the use of OTA agreements in DoD outsourcing. Both are written and provided by Richard L. Dunn, first general counsel at DARPA, 1987–2000, and founder and consultant of the Strategic Institute FOR Innovation in Government Contracting. I have lightly edited both.[61]

Digital Gallium Arsenide Microprocessors

In 1989 DARPA initiated the insertion phase of its long-standing work with digital gallium arsenide microprocessors. The insertion program was undertaken because of the potential advantages of using these microprocessors in military systems that were displayed in early DARPA-funded research. According to a DoD press release at the time:

> Digital gallium arsenide devices are particularly well suited for military systems because they consume a fraction of the power, operate at much higher speeds, function over wider temperature range and are much more resistant to radiation than silicon components. Although GaAs chips typically cost more than the silicon components they replace, their greater performance can lead to cost savings because fewer components are necessary to implement a particular function.
>
> By 1950 earlier work on semi-conductors led to the practical application of the transistor as a substitute for the vacuum tube in electronics. Original semi-conductor materials were germanium and silicon with silicon eventually becoming dominant. In the 1950's the transistor radio became ubiquitous. By the end of the decade another major advance was the invention of an integrated circuit. This was followed by the micro-processor. While these advances were taking place exploratory research on other materials that might be used in semi-conductor applications took place. Among these materials was GaAs.

DARPA (then ARPA) was an early sponsor of digital gallium arsenide microprocessor research initially with a view to application in space operations. As a compound semiconductor, these microprocessors presented problems in basic development. Once these were addressed, problems in fabrication arose. Because these microprocessors were more expensive than silicon microprocessors and offered little if any potential advantage over silicon for commercial applications, private investment was not attracted to this research. In addition to long-term support from DARPA, the military services episodically sponsored such research. The actual research was conducted by firms in the defense industry.

The mid-1960s saw the first digital gallium arsenide microprocessor device, a field effect transistor (FET). Fairchild produced a microwave FET while other research took place at the Center for Materials Research, established by DARPA at Stanford University. Companies involved in digital gallium arsenide microprocessor research included Hewlett-Packard, Hughes, McDonnell-Douglas, Rockwell, and Texas Instruments.

In the 1980s, DARPA created a joint program supported by its Strategic Technologies Office (whose interests included space applications) and the Defense Sciences Office (center of DARPA materials research). In the mid-1980s, pilot chip production lines were set up at Rockwell and McDonnell-Douglas. It was recognized that for digital gallium arsenide microprocessor to reach goals for application in an advanced onboard signal processor, both complexity of devices and yield would need to be increased by orders of magnitude. Meanwhile Rockwell envisioned the potential for commercial applications and spun off two companies, Gigabit Logic (1981) and Vitesse Semiconductors (1984), to address commercial or dual-use products. These companies along with TriQuint Semiconductor, specializing in radiofrequency applications as well as chip production, received DARPA research funding. With DARPA's "seal of approval," they were also able to attract private investment. TriQuint worked with gallium nitride as well as digital gallium arsenide. TriQuint provided digital gallium arsenide chips to startup company Gazelle Microcircuits, which, in 1989, at the time DARPA's insertion program began, was entirely supported by venture capital. Its venture capital investment no doubt was partly attributable to glow from DARPA support for Gigabit and Vitesse.

Gazelle became an asset to DARPA's insertion program in an unusual way. Gazelle was developing transmitter and receiver chips operating at one gigabit per second or faster. Just as Gazelle's venture capital funding was running dry, DARPA was able to step in and provide funding quickly and without the overhead and burden usually associated with government funding. Gazelle received funding under the first OTA awarded pursuant to DARPA's new authority (10 US Code 2371).

In less than a year after agreement award, Gazelle chips provided key capabilities to (1) a major defense company's infrared and radar processing systems; (2) a national laboratory's transmission of nuclear test data over fiber-optic cable with no transmission errors; (3) a network of transputers and custom processors to a Canadian firm developing processors for antisubmarine warfare, synthetic aperture radar, and sensor fusion targeting applications; (4) a major defense company's computer-to-computer interconnection-across-fiber project; (5) a major defense company's classified program; and (6) a complex integrated broadband network involving DARPA, the National Science Foundation, as well as many research universities and defense and commercial companies.

It was found that if Gazelle's high-speed chips were not available as standard parts, custom or application-specific circuits would have to be designed to carry out the transmitter and receiver functions. Such an undertaking would result in greater cost for the project as well as schedule delays.

Just a year after receiving the first OTA agreement, Gazelle merged with Gigabit Logic and TriQuint to form a new TriQuint. In 2015, TriQuint engaged in another merger that resulted in the creation of Qorvo. Qorvo is a world leader in digital gallium arsenide microprocessors and gallium nitride radiofrequency products, including products that support 5G applications. Most smart phones and cell phone base stations contain Qorvo components. Major Chinese and South Korean companies are among Qorvo's customers. High-technology sales in the right direction.

The Commercial Operations and Support Savings Initiative

Because defense systems cost too much and take too long to field, DoD tends not to refresh or replace its systems on a timely basis.

Instead, legacy systems remain operational for decades, sometimes many decades. This in turn results in systems and their components remaining in service long after production has ended. When necessary spare parts are needed but out of production, serious problems can be encountered. First is simply the time and cost involved in restarting a production line in order to provide the parts needed to maintain the system. The mere idea of starting a production line to build obsolete parts is amazing in itself. Another problem is that as a result of turbulence in the defense industrial base since the end of the Cold War, many former defense contractors are no longer in business. These defunct companies may own the intellectual property rights (e.g., patents, technical data) necessary for production.

With the creation of the Commercial Operations and Support Savings Initiative (COSSI), the essential idea was to replace the obsolete component with a commercially available part that has been modified and qualified to do the same job as the obsolete part in an affordable and often superior manner.

The goals of COSSI were to improve readiness and reduce operation and support costs by inserting existing commercial items or technology into military legacy systems. COSSI emphasized the rapid development of prototypes and fielding of production items based on current commercial technology. The program also implemented the goals: (1) expand the use of commercial practices and products that will facilitate the modernization of military forces; (2) improve the acquisition process; and (3) make near-term investments to acquire modern capabilities based upon US scientific and industrial preeminence.

COSSI funding leveraged technology developments made by commercial firms, reducing research and development costs for DoD. OTAs were used in the first phase so that participation in COSSI would be attractive to commercial firms. They would not need to adopt costly defense-specific business practices in order to participate in the program. Projects might be fully funded by the government or in some cases cost-shared with private industry.

COSSI involved a two-stage process. In the first stage, dedicated COSSI R&D funds were used to perform the nonrecurring engineering, testing, and qualification that are typically needed to adapt a commercial item/technology for use in a military system. Selected contractors develop, fabricate, and deliver a prototype "kit" to a military customer for installation into a fielded DoD system. Each prototype kit consisted of a commercial item, or a combination of commercial items, that were adapted, qualification-tested, and readied for insertion. The first stage typically lasted for months or a year or more. The second stage involved the purchase of production quantities of the prototype kits, typically as FAR commercial items.

Between fiscal years 1997 and 2000, seventy-seven projects were funded through the program. COSSI contributed an investment of $234 million, and contractor spending contributed another $143 million. The projected operations and support cost savings for thirty projects from fiscal years 1997 and 1999 that transitioned or were in process of transitioning into the second stage was over $5 billion. Subsequent net present value analysis over four years established that thirty-six operations and maintenance (O&M) dollars were saved for each R&D dollar invested.

Although COSSI established a record of success, it also encountered a number of challenges. These included some organizations requiring a competition rather than awarding a sole source production contract after successful demonstration of the qualified "kit." In some cases, production funds that had been promised were not forthcoming. Finally, when COSSI no longer had a dedicated line of centrally managed R&D funding, the military departments failed to prioritize their own R&D funding to continue the program and it fell into disuse, with only a remnant of its technique remaining.

As can be seen from this brief discussion, COSSI serves as a model not only for replacing obsolete, out-of-production components but also for gaining the cost and scheduling advantages of leveraging commercial developments and investments. Today DoD has the opportunity not only to replicate COSSI to solve a serious problem but also to improve on the COSSI model. Thanks to Congress a successful OTA prototype project can transition to follow-on production on a commercially friendly basis. Follow-on production can take place under a modification to the prototype OTA, under a production OTA, or as a sole-source FAR contract.

The COSSI model is merely a starting position for innovation. COSSI used R&D funds in the first phase, but for system upgrades

O&M might also be used. The second phase might be funded with either O&M or procurement funds. Industry can be encouraged for nonrecurring engineering and qualification of the replacement kit.

From the above case studies it should be apparent that in utilizing OTAs, DoD was able to bring in new firms, stimulate the development of new defense-relevant technology, and use a relatively small amount of DoD funds to generate private investment, including from venture capital—in sum, with a small sum, to generate a large output. All of this required much more flexibility than traditional FAR authorities would allow. Indeed, what is missing from OTAs includes the following: Competition in Contracting Act; Truthful Cost and Pricing Act; Cost Accounting Standards; Contract Disputes Act; Buy America Act; Bayh-Dole Act; Procurement Protest System; and Service Contract Act.[62] What is clear from the definitive statement on what OTAs are, and are not, is the need for flexibility and innovative thinking.[63]

Incentives

The topic of incentives was raised in the 2014 annual report of DoD on acquisitions.[64] That report noted the theory of incentives of Chester Barnard in *The Functions of the Executive*, first published in 1938, in which there are two chapters dealing with incentives.[65] In "The Economy of Incentives" he states:

> An essential element of organizations is the willingness of persons to contribute their individual efforts to the cooperative system.... Inadequate incentives mean dissolution, or changes of organization purpose, or failure to cooperate. Hence, in all sorts of organizations the affording of adequate incentives becomes the most definitely emphasized task in their existence. It is probably in this aspect of executive work that failure is most pronounced.[66]

The incentives may be specific or general:

> The specific inducements that may be offered are of several classes, for example: a) material inducements; b) personal nonmaterial opportunities; c) desirable physical conditions; d) ideal benefactions. General incentives afforded are, for example: e) associational attractiveness; f) adaptation of conditions to habitual methods and

attitudes; g) opportunity of enlarged participation; h) the condition of communion.[67]

In short, from the beginning of development of theories of incentives with Barnard, there is recognition that incentives are not only material, but also extend to nonmaterial, and beyond.[68] The issue of incentives, or lack thereof, was a continuing theme in my interviews and is also noted in some of the scholarly work on the topic of contracting-out.[69]

It would be easy to draw from a fairly extensive and robust scholarly literature on theories of incentives. I believe, however, that this is not necessary, since from my experience in DoD for a quarter century, my research on outsourcing, and my personal contacts with contracting officers and with the "industry," I am aware of very few incentives for contracting officers to do anything but adhere to the security blanket provided by the FAR. As noted in Chapter 1, their salaries, especially relative to contractors, are not competitive. There are few, if any, nonmaterial incentives. The A-76 process illustrates a sense or belief in the United States that government employment is parasitic. Indeed, according to highly regarded survey research by the Pew Research Center in a September 2020 report, just 20 percent of the population said they trust the government in Washington, DC, to do the right thing always or most of the time.[70] Instead of incentives to innovate, and utilize OTAs, there are obvious disincentives, the most dramatic of which is being fired.

It is general knowledge that one of the first things a contracting officer hears is: "Stick with the FAR. It will keep you out of jail." A review of the responsibilities of a CO, by the Federal Acquisition Institute, which was created to foster and promote the development of a federal acquisition workforce, must be unsettling for anyone working for DoD, as the review is very scary in its scope and implications. The FAQs stipulate that COs are responsible for ensuring the following:[71]

- The Government obtains value from contracts
- All requirements of law and regulation are met prior to executing an action
- Sufficient funds are available for obligation

- Contractors receive impartial, fair, and equitable treatment
- Both parties comply with terms of the contract
- The interests of the United States are safeguarded and taxpayer's money is spent wisely

If accused, how can a CO prove to investigators that he or she has fulfilled all these responsibilities? Anyone at all familiar with the ever-changing nature and complexity of policy and official documents in DoD and the armed services can understand why COs are averse to taking any risk. The experience of the DIU and of DARPA, both of which use OTAs, is an important contrast. These organizations have personnel who are well versed in the use of OTAs and have invested in having senior advisors to work with their staff in negotiating OTAs.[72] It is no accident that the two case studies presented in this chapter were DARPA initiatives.[73]

There is a commonly held suspicion that military contracting officers on retirement move into positions in the industry where they can use their knowledge of (and contacts in DoD) to win contracts and receive much higher salaries. J. Ronald Fox, probably the foremost academic expert on outsourcing, states the following in his classic book:

> Despite the urgent need for competent acquisition managers within the military, there are at present few incentives for qualified officers to remain in the service after 20 years. The defense industry, on the other hand, provides a compelling incentive for a knowledgeable officer to leave the service: rewarding salary scale and career status. . . . Positions are offered to officers who have demonstrated their appreciation for industry's particular problems and commitments.[74]

Unfortunately, all the "data" are anecdotal, and I cannot imagine how it can ever be proven empirically.[75]

Experts in government contracting provide evidence of a tendency to make bulletproof contracting vehicles. One piece of evidence is the fact that FAR regulations on commercial items in their original form allowed great flexibility. Between 1994 and today, 154 articles have been added to those regulations that have eliminated this flexibility.[76] There is a concern, which is conveyed very clearly in the Center for Government Contracting podcast and in the report by Soloway, Knudson, and Wroble, that OTAs will increasingly undergo what they refer to as "FAR creep."[77]

While the term "oversight" has for most people a positive connotation, it must be stated that synonyms include "control" and "surveillance." A CO has absolutely no incentive to be flexible, take chances, use OTAs if he or she cannot be sure, as he or she never can, that some higher level will not conduct an audit, or worse yet, an inspector general team will not look kindly on the flexibility offered by using an OTA. In a worst-case scenario, with which I am very familiar, the Naval Criminal Investigative Service can be called in to gather evidence for a criminal proceeding. In sum, considering the federal pay cap, COs have little incentive to excel, and utilize OTAs, since, as a common phrase in DoD is "No good deed goes unpunished" and as promotion is very unlikely, if there is anything that can result in being fired by DoD and the services, it is precisely the financial issues summarized in the CO "responsibilities" listed earlier.

Implementation

The February 22, 2019, CRS report by Heidi M. Peters, in addition to citing potential benefits of using OTAs, also lists potential risks and notes that Congress has at times expressed concerns that OTs could be used to circumvent congressional intent. She cites the 1999 NDAA as well as the 2019 NDAA that makes this same point. The 2019 NDAA clarified the reporting requirements, and this was reiterated in the 2020 NDAA. While this CRS report raised the possibility that Congress could "clamp down" on the authority, in fact the 2021 NDAA did not do so.[78] A GAO report on OTAs in 2016, in its summary, states the following: "This authority [OTA] carries risk, however, because such agreements may be exempt from the Federal Acquisition Regulation and other requirements that are intended to protect taxpayer's interests."[79]

The concept and issue of accountability regarding the use of OTAs had been brought up much earlier, before they began to catch on at all with DoD. For example, the title of a hearing in the House of Representatives on February 7, 2008, on the use of OTAs in the

Department of Homeland Security was "Other Transaction Authority: Flexibility at the Expense of Accountability?" The overall conclusion of the experts who testified at the hearing from the Department of Homeland Security, Congressional Research Service, and Government Accountability Office was positive about the use of OTAs.[80] More recently, on March 15, 2019, the Project on Government Oversight published a report with the title "Other Transactions: Do the Rewards Outweigh the Risks?"[81] Its conclusion is that no, the rewards do not outweigh the risks. I fundamentally disagree with this report, for three reasons. First, the basic statement that the US government is at the mercy of contractors is asserted rather than proved. Second, while the report's data on the participation of nontraditional contractors may have been accurate in the past, it is not now. According to Undersecretary of Defense for Acquisition and Sustainment Ellen Lord in fiscal year 2019: "88% of OTA business is with companies who typically did not do business previously with the government."[82] And third, the report recommends using the FAR, which would negate the whole purpose of OTAs, which is speed in acquisitions.[83]

Conclusion

My research on the use of OTAs by DoD has led me to not one but four conclusions. First, as clearly demonstrated by the huge and timely infusion of money into the purchase of equipment and development and production of vaccines to combat Covid-19, OTAs can be very successfully employed for quick results. Second, consortia appear to be more popular than attempting to work with startups in Silicon Valley in bringing new, military-relevant technology to DoD. Third is the need for more information on the use OTAs to avoid their misuse and to best tailor them to the most pressing needs of DoD for advanced technology. The awareness of this need is seen clearly in the emphasis of several NDAAs on reporting and the most recent GAO report.[84] This need is a constant theme in the GAO and is found in the NDAA for fiscal year 2022. The title of one GAO annual report says it all: "Defense Acquisitions Annual Assessment: Drive to Deliver Capabilities Faster Increases Importance of Program Knowledge and Consistent

Data for Oversight."[85] Fourth, given the tremendous leeway of the "agreement officer" in including, or excluding, requirements, there is need to change the mentality or culture of COs into that of "agreement officers." There are, however, huge disincentives for the COs to break away from the security blanket of the FAR.

Notes

1. GAO, "Military Acquisitions" (Washington, DC, July 2017) pp. 5, 27.
2. Ash Carter, *Inside the Five-Sided Box: Lessons from a Lifetime of Leadership in the Pentagon* (New York: Dutton, 2019), p. 327.
3. See https://www.diu.mil/about.
4. Quoted in William J. Weinig, "Other Transaction Authority: Saints or Sinner for Defense Acquisitions?" *Defense Acquisition Research Journal* 26, no. 2 (April 2019): p. 114. Christian Brose devotes two chapters to the importance of Silicon Valley for US national security: *The Kill Chain: Defending America in the Future of High-Tech Warfare* (New York: Hachette, 2020). And most recently, the DoD Office of Net Assessment sponsored the report by Nathan Voss and James Ryseff, *Comparing the Organizational Cultures of the Department of Defense and Silicon Valley* (Santa Monica: RAND, 2022).
5. "The New Grand Bargain," *The Economist*, November 21, 2020, p. 19. The tech giants are Apple, followed by Alphabet, Facebook, and Amazon.
6. As discussed by Zegart in her podcast with the Council on Foreign Relations, November 20, 2019, https://www.cfr.org/conference-calls/national-security-and-silicon-valley.
7. I lived in Silicon Valley for five years, and for forty years I lived within one hour's drive to Silicon Valley. In these comments, I draw on my personal experience; on an excellent book by Margaret O'Mara, *The Code: Silicon Valley and the Remaking of America* (New York: Penguin, 2019); and on the *New York Times* reporting on the trial of the founder of Theranos, Elizabeth Holmes, in the US District Court of Northern California in the fall and winter of 2021.
8. I have found the DIU's "Annual Report, FY 2021" extremely useful: https://www.diu.mil/latest/diu-fy-2021-annual-report-a-preview-into-fy-2022. In early May 2022, Michael Brown reported that he would not seek to renew his appointment as director of DIU, alleging that DoD is not moving fast enough in incorporating commercially available technologies into the acquisition process. This was reported widely in *Politico* and trade publications including *Breaking Defense* and *Defense News* at that time.

9. One source estimated that there were between 6,000 and 9,000 startups in Silicon Valley and nearby San Francisco in November 2018; see https://www.quora.com/How-many-tech-startups-are-there-in-San-Francisco-and-Silicon-Valley-with-more-than-five-employees. The most recent assessment of venture capital is as follows: "A booming ecosystem of highly valued, cash-rich startups in Silicon Valley and beyond that are expanding at break-neck speed and trying to unseat stalwart companies in all kinds of fields"; Erin Griffith, "The Relentless Fever for Tech Start-Ups," *New York Times*, January 20, 2022, p. B5. The most positive assessment I have seen is that 50 percent of startups in Silicon Valley survive; https://www.forbes.com/sites/forbestechcouncil/2018/06/15/silicon-valleys-secret-ingredient-to-startup-success/?sh=518dea6d6049.

10. Rachel Olney, "The Rift Between Silicon Valley and the Pentagon Is Economic, Not Moral," *War on the Rocks*, January 28, 2018.

11. Weinig, "Other Transaction Authority," p. 113. In order to be balanced, I would be remiss if I didn't cite a contrary, legal perspective on the use of OTAs: Jerome Gabig and Richard Raleigh, "Debunking the Hype Involving 'Other Transaction Authority,'" *Contract Management*, March 2019, pp. 43–51.

12. Heidi M. Peters, "Department of Defense Use of Other Transaction Authority: Background, Analysis, and Issues for Congress" (Washington, DC: Congressional Research Service, February 22, 2019), p. 1. Emphasis added.

13. For this summary, I draw on Peters, "Department of Defense Use of Other Transaction Authority"; GAO, "Covid-19 Contracting: Actions Needed" (Washington, DC, July 2021); Office of the Undersecretary of Defense for Acquisition and Sustainment, https://www.dau.edu/guidebooks/Shared%20Documents/Other%20Transactions%20(OT)%20Guide.pdf; GovWin IQ (from Deltec) briefing, February 10, 2021; Benjamin Schwartz and Bill Greenwalt, "Other Transaction Authority and the Consortia-Based Acquisition Model: A Valuable Tool for Rapid Defense Innovation" (Washington, DC: Chertoff Group, 2020); and Strategic Institute FOR Innovation in Government Contracting, *Guide to Other Transactions Authority*, 3rd ed. (Washington, DC, 2021).

14. Stan Soloway, Jason Knudson, and Vincent Wroble, "Other Transactions Authorities: After 60 Years, Hitting Their Stride or Hitting the Wall?" (Washington, DC: IBM Center for the Business of Government, 2021), p. 6.

15. Peters, "Department of Defense Use of Other Transaction Authority," p. 3.

16. GAO, "DOD's Use of Other Transactions for Prototype Projects Has Increased" (Washington, DC, November 2019).

17. Lauren A. Mayer et al., "Prototyping Using Other Transactions: Case Studies for the Acquisition Community": (Santa Monica: RAND, 2020), "Recommendations," p. xi.

18. Ibid., pp. 17–25. Reiterated in Center for Government Contracting, George Mason University, December 9, 2021, podcast, https://business.gmu.edu/govcon/webinars-podcasts-and-virtual-networking-events/.

19. Peters, "Department of Defense Use of Other Transaction Authority," p. 6.

20. Office of the Undersecretary of Defense for Acquisition and Sustainment, "Other Transactions Guide" (Washington, DC, November 2018), p. 4. More recently, in US Department of Defense, "State of Competition Within the Defense Industrial Base," DoD specifically highlighted the importance of OTAs in broadening the industrial base (p. 13).

21. In addition, the most recent and comprehensive report on OTAs details the importance of the Covid response to DoD's increasing use of OTAs. See Rhys McCormick and Gregory Sanders, *Trends in Department of Defense Other Transaction Authority Usage* (Lanham: Rowman and Littlefield, May 2022).

22. GAO, "Covid-19 Contracting: Observations on Federal Contracting in Response to the Pandemic" (Washington, DC, July 2020), "Highlights."

23. GAO, "Covid-19 Contracting: Actions Needed to Enhance Transparency and Oversight of Selected Awards" (Washington, DC, July 2021), "Highlights."

24. GAO, "Covid-19 Contracting: Observations," p. 22.

25. Ibid., pp. 22–23.

26. GAO, "Covid-19 Contracting: Actions Needed," pp. 27–29.

27. See, for example, Paul Sonne, "How a Secretive Pentagon Agency Seeded the Ground for a Rapid Coronavirus Cure," *Washington Post*, July 30, 2020.

28. GAO 21-501, p. 32.

29. Stan Soloway in the Center for Government Contracting podcast. Soloway also noted that the NDAA for fiscal year 2021 requested a catalogue of consortia.

30. See, for example, https://www.dau.edu/cop/ot/Lists/Related%20Websites/DispForm.aspx?ID=7&ContentTypeId=0x010500F192002DF5AC9D43ADC3A367DD687C1001009D9B7691427A044CBCE77EF9FA36544C. For further information on consortia, see "Other Transactions and Other Transaction Consortia," https://aida.mitre.org/demystifying-dod/ots-otconsortia. It must be noted, however, that according to Richard L. Dunn of the Strategic Institute FOR Innovation in Government Contracting, consortia may not fit within the sense or philosophy behind the use of OTAs. See Strategic Institute FOR Innovation in Government Contracting, *Guide to Other Transactions Authority*, pp. 65–67.

31. It should be noted, however, that the Strategic Institute FOR Innovation in Government Contracting has a podcast that raises questions about the consortia model. See https://strategicinstitute.org. The authors in the

most recent analysis identify forty-two consortia, thirty-eight in DoD. See Moshe Schwartz and Stephanie Halcrow, "The Power of Many: Leveraging Consortia to Promote Innovation, Expand the Defense Industrial Base, and Accelerate Innovation," (Fairfax County, VA: George Mason University Center for Government Contracting, July 18, 2022).

32. Michael H. Cecire, "Covid-19 and Domestic PPE Production and Distribution: Issues and Policy Options" (Washington, DC: Congressional Research Service, December 7, 2020), pp. 47–48.

33. This problem is analyzed in Brazil in Thomas Bruneau and Florina Cristiana Matei, "Brazil: The Ebb and Flow of Democratic Civilian Control," in Florina Cristiana Matei, Carolyn Halladay, and Thomas Bruneau, eds., *The Routledge Handbook of Civil-Military Relations*, 2nd ed. (London: Routledge, 2021).

34. That this issue is not a problem in the United States can be seen in David Pion-Berlin, Thomas Bruneau, and Richard B. Goetze Jr., "The Trump Self-Coup Attempt: Comparisons and Civil-Military Relations," *Government and Opposition* (2022), pp. 1–18.

35. CSIS, "Maintaining the Intelligence Edge" (Washington, DC, January 2021), p. x. Emphasis in original.

36. Ibid., p. 24.

37. House Permanent Select Committee on Intelligence, *Rightly Scaled, Carefully Open, Infinitely Agile: Reconfiguring to Win the Innovation Race in the Intelligence Community* (Washington, DC, 2020), https://intelligence.house.gov/uploadedfiles/final_start_report_v4.pdf.

38. Ibid., p. 28.

39. CSIS, "Maintaining the Intelligence Edge," p. 27.

40. Ibid., p. 28.

41. Ibid., p. 30.

42. Ibid., p. 53. Emphasis in original.

43. Richard Dunn, "2021 NDAA: All Systems GO for Other Transactions! But Curiosity About So-Called 'Consortia'" (Florida: Strategic Institute FOR Innovation in Government Contracting, January 28, 2021), https://strategicinstitute.org.

44. The Office of the Secretary of Defense published a timeline with fourteen subsequent congressional expansions of OTAs: https://www.transform.af.mil/Portals/18/documents/OTA/OTA%20Statutory%20Timeline.pdf?ver=2018-02-07-165325-513.

45. Geoff Merritt and Shohei Takagi, "The Ins & Outs of Other Transaction Agreements (OTAs)" (Arlington, VA: BDO, September 17, 2020), slide 16. This is the US segment of the international firm Binder, Dijker Otte. Emphasis added. Copy in possession of the author.

46. Weinig, "Other Transaction Authority," p. 116. Crane Lopes, "Historical Institutionalism and Defense Public Procurement: The Case of

Other Transactions Agreements," dissertation, September 19, 2018, goes into great detail on the support of Congress in several NDAAs for the use of OTAs by DoD. Most recently, for Center for Government Contracting, Stan Soloway states that in his interviews with staff and members in Congress, they are very positive about the use of OTAs.

47. Email communication from Richard Beutel of Cyrrus Analytics LLC, September 14, 2020.

48. Peters, "Department of Defense Use of Other Transaction Authority," "Summary."

49. Fiscal year 2022 NDAA, p. 179.

50. See https://www.congress.gov/115/crpt/hrpt404/CRPT-115hrpt404.pdf.

51. Lopes, "Historical Institutionalism and Defense Public Procurement," p. 34.

52. Ibid., p. 33.

53. Ibid., p. 622.

54. Ibid.

55. See https://strategicinstitute.org/other-transactions/2021-ndaa-ota. He stated the same in an email to me dated October 12, 2020. My research indicates that there is one professor at Defense Acquisition University who has expertise in OTAs. According to GAO, "Defense Workforce: Steps Needed to Identify Acquisition Training Needs for Non-Acquisition Personnel" (Washington, DC, September 2019), p. 7, the university has 600 faculty and staff. I was informed on June 13, 2022, that the faculty member with expertise in OTAs had left the university for "industry."

56. See http://icatalog.dau.mil and https://www.acq.osd.mil/dpap/cpic/cp/10usc2371bots.html. Despite several efforts to communicate with instructors at Defense Acquisition University, I never received a response regarding education or training in the use of OTAs.

57. CSIS, "Maintaining the Intelligence Edge," p. 53. Emphasis in original.

58. Available at https://nsarchive.gwu.edu/sites/default/files/documents/r07q93-i4vtr/001.pdf. Emphasis added.

59. Available at https://federalnewsnetwork.com/on-dod/2021/11/amid-explosion-in-dods-use-of-otas-myths-abound-about-how-and-whether-to-use-them. The figure of $16.2 billion is also used in McCormick and Sanders, *Trends in Department of Defense Other Transaction Authority Usage*, p. 48.

60. The three most empirical studies—that is, those at least partly based on interview data—are Lopes, "Historical Institutionalism and Defense Public Procurement," p. 237; Mayer, "Prototyping Using Other Transactions," p. xi; and Soloway, Knudson, and Wroble, "Other Transactions Authorities," focus on workforce issues as an explanation for the lack of adoption of OTAs. The first two use the term "risk-averse" regarding COs.

61. For another six case studies, see Strategic Institute FOR Innovation in Government Contracting, *Guide to Other Transactions Authority.*

62. Taken from Merritt and Takagi, "The Ins & Outs of Other Transaction Agreements (OTAs)," webinar, September 17, 2020, presented for Deltec by BDO, p. 11. Copy of slides are in my possession.

63. Most emphatically stated in Strategic Institute FOR Innovation in Government Contracting, *Guide to Other Transactions Authority,* passim.

64. Undersecretary of Defense for Acquisition, Technology, and Logistics, "Performance of the Defense Acquisition System 2014 Annual Report" (Washington, DC: USD[AT&L], June 13, 2014), p. 4, https://www.acq.osd.mil/fo/docs/Performance-of-Defense-Acquisition-System-2014.pdf. The issue of negative, or perverse, incentives is identified by Michael J. Sullivan, director, acquisition and sourcing management; GAO, "Defense Acquisition: Addressing Incentives Is Key to Further Reform Efforts," testimony before the Senate Committee on Armed Services, April 30, 2014.

65. Chester Barnard, *The Functions of the Executive* (Cambridge: Harvard University Press, 1962 [originally published 1938]).

66. Ibid., p. 139.

67. Ibid., p. 142.

68. The most complete discussion I have seen on incentives, in this case leading up to principal-agent theories, is Jean-Jacques Laffont and David Martifort, *The Theory of Incentives I: The Principal-Agent Model* (Princeton: Princeton University Press, 2002).

69. The lack of financial incentives for government employees is a central theme in Paul C. Light, *A Government Ill Executed: The Decline of the Federal Service and How to Reverse It* (Cambridge: Harvard University Press, 2008). This fact is recognized in at least one book on private security contractors. Stanger writes that "government's human capital crisis follows from the diminished attractiveness of low-paying government positions when comparable work in the private sector is available at higher pay"; Allison Stanger, *One Nation Under Contract: The Outsourcing of American Power and the Future of Foreign Policy* (New Haven: Yale University Press, 2009), p. 17.

70. See https://www.pewresearch.org/politics/2020/09/14/americans-views-of-government-low-trust-but-some-positive-performance-ratings.

71. Listed in "Frequently Asked Questions (FAQ) About Government Contracting Careers," https://www.fai.gov/sites/default/files/Questions%20for%20new%20contacting%20professionals.pdf.

72. This was stated clearly by Wes Bennett, director of the Contract Management Office at DARPA in the Center for Government Contracts, and by Bill Greenwald for the DIU in the Center for Strategic and International Studies, September 23, 2021, podcasts, https://business.gmu.edu/govcon/webinars-podcasts-and-virtual-networking-events/ and https://www.csis.org/events/connecting-us-innovation-ecosystem-national-security.

73. The more likely scenario is conveyed by the following from a Defense Acquisition University description of 4023 (previously U.S.C. 2373: "Pursuit and execution of this provision for purchases, especially when used in combination with an OT, requires highly experienced and empowered staff; lack of guidance, structure, and processes can challenge and intimidate inexperienced staff"; https://aaf.dau.edu/aaf/contracting-cone.

74. J. Ronald Fox, *Arming America: How the U.S. Buys Weapons* (Boston: Harvard University Press, 1974), pp. 460–464.

75. I tried, but despite my best efforts, it has proven impossible to obtain credible data on the movement of military contracting officers to the private sector. I tried by co-supervising a thesis by students in the Acquisition Management Curriculum at NPS. While the Defense Manpower Data Center, located in Monterey, California, has the data, it is confidential. And my efforts to obtain the data were stymied by the Institutional Review Board at NPS. I can conceive of no database that would provide data on civilian contracting officers working for DoD to move to "the industry."

76. Stated by Stan Soloway in Center for Government Contracting podcast, December 9, 2021. Regarding the recommendations of the 809 Panel to remedy this situation, see Soloway, Knudson, and Wroble, "Other Transactions Authorities," pp. 43–44.

77. Soloway, Knudson, and Wroble, "Other Transactions Authorities," p. 41.

78. Peters, "Department of Defense Use of Other Transaction Authority," pp. 8–9, regarding the possibility of "clamping down."

79. GAO, "Federal Acquisitions: Use of 'Other Transaction' Agreements Limited and Mostly for Research and Development Activities" (Washington, DC, January 7, 2016).

80. "Other Transaction Authority: Flexibility at the Expense of Accountability?" hearing before the Subcommittee on Emerging Threats, Cybersecurity, and Science and Technology of the House Committee on Homeland Security, February 7, 2008; https://www.govinfo.gov/content/pkg/CHRG-110hhrg44511/html/CHRG-110hhrg44511.htm.

81. Available at https://www.pogo.org/report/2019/03/other-transactions-do-the-rewards-outweigh-the-risks.

82. Available at https://www.governmentcontractslegalforum.com/2019/12/articles/legal-developments/dod-acquisition-chief-looks-back-at-the-year-that-was-and-previews-the-year-to-come. This point is further emphasized as follows: "The data show that nearly 96 percent of DoD OTA obligations were awarded to nontraditional significant participation, looking at the data by top vendors shows that most DoD OTA obligations are awarded to consortia"; Rhys McCormick, "Defense Acquisition Trends 2020: Topline DoD Trends" (Washington, DC: CSIS, October 2020), p. 7. This point becomes particularly relevant when we recall that the five largest DoD contractors by obligation in fiscal year 2020 received 54 percent of all

DoD contract obligations; *CRS In Focus,* "Defense Primer: Department of Defense Contractors" (Washington, DC, December 17, 2021).

83. POGO report, p. 13, https://www.pogo.org/report/2019/03/other-transactions-do-the-rewards-outweigh-the-risks.

84. GAO, "Army Should Improve Use of Alternative Agreements and Approaches by Enhancing Oversight and Communication of Lessons Learned" (Washington, DC, October 2020).

85. GAO, "Defense Acquisitions Annual Assessment: Drive to Deliver Capabilities Faster Increases Importance of Program Knowledge and Consistent Data for Oversight" (Washington, DC, June 2020).

7

Public Money, Private Gains

THIS BOOK SEEKS TO CONTRIBUTE TO TWO AREAS. FIRST, TO THE STUDY of civil-military relations by analyzing the outsourcing of security. The book focuses on the authorities, or legal frameworks, for contracting-out, since the contract is the sine qua non for the 10 million contracts awarded by DoD annually as referred to by Secretary of Defense Ash Carter. Considering the number of contracts, the financial scale of outsourcing, which is more than half of the roughly $760 billion DoD annual budget, and the half a million full-time contract employees, it is impossible to analyze US national defense and security policy without including the dimension of contracting-out. At a minimum, to replace those half million contract employees would most likely require half a million uniformed personnel, something unlikely to happen without mandatory conscription, which would cause gigantic problems in civil-military relations. Second, the book seeks to contribute to the analysis of outsourcing, without which the first goal cannot be achieved. Precisely because of the scale and complexity of the phenomenon, and the exclusive focus on outsourcing by acquisition specialists, however, there is virtually no social science literature on the general topic and, therefore, no accepted framework for analysis. In order to organize and make sense of the widely disparate information, I employed a modified framework developed for the analysis of civil-military relations, expanded to include effectiveness in addition to control. The sources of information include all the written material I could find (which has resulted in six full banker boxes and untold numbers of electronic files) as well as more than sixty personal interviews, several of them more than once.

Summary

Chapter 2 sought to demonstrate that security has been periodically privatized since the founding of the American republic, and that the current laws and policy strongly encourage privatization. The A-76 process epitomizes the emphasis on privatization of everything in the United States, including security. The fact that the process is currently "suspended" suggests early on in the book that there is a political dimension to outsourcing, or in this case, not outsourcing.

Chapter 3 focused on what is commonly called "expeditionary contracting" and more specifically on the wars in Afghanistan and Iraq. In analyzing operational contract support and private security contractors, the chapter sought to convey that large sums of money and great numbers of contractors were involved, and there were just as many problems. There is virtually unanimous agreement that the root cause of the problems, and ultimately the failure of US policy in both countries, was the lack of a strategy that could guide policy, including outsourcing. In fact, in line with my framework for analysis, nothing was right with expeditionary contracting in Afghanistan and Iraq. The FAR was not followed, Congress did not implement most of the recommendations of the Commission on Wartime Contracting in Iraq and Afghanistan, the education/training of non-acquisition officers was never implemented, there was a shortage of COs, and CORs were not adequately prepared. Considering the mess regarding contingency contracting, it is not surprising that neither Afghanistan nor Iraq can be considered successful in either US foreign or security policy.

Chapter 4 dealt with the topic of outsourcing secret intelligence. Given the background of the intelligence community at the end of the Cold War, with the inception of the global war on terrorism after 9/11 the IC had to outsource for cleared or clearable personnel for access to secret information. This process led to very serious problems, epitomized by Abu Ghraib and the Snowden affair. The problem was, however, overcome due to the forceful involvement of Congress, the creation of the ODNI, and the implementation of personnel policies across the IC. That problem, concerning personnel, was resolved. Whether or not the IC is effective is unknowable, since intelligence is a service for decisionmakers, and whether the decisionmakers follow the intelligence or not is unknowable to all but the decisionmakers themselves.

Chapter 5 provided the background for the reorientation of US policy from the global war on terrorism, which was never a strategy in any case, to great power competition, which, under Secretary of Defense Mattis, became a strategy and continues to be promoted by the US government, including Congress, with laws and funding. The reorientation to great power competition, in the context of disregard for research and development of advanced military technologies after the end of the Cold War and during the global war on terrorism, has led to calls for more flexible acquisition authorities than available in the FAR. The main problem with the current acquisition system, based on the FAR, is not what could be defined as disasters, but rather opportunity costs that can only be fully understood if there are hostilities, which if they occur will most likely be with China.

Chapter 6 focused on an alternative acquisition authority, OTAs, the value of which was proven in the discovery and production of anti-Covid-19 vaccines and personal protective equipment. Considering the recognized success in the use of OTAs by the DIU and in responding to the Covid pandemic, however, the growth in the use of OTAs is modest. It is hypothesized that this is due to concern by COs that they may be vulnerable for their actions if not "covered" by the FAR. Then, too, OTAs require a great deal of awareness and knowledge on the part of the COs, termed agreement officers. I argue that contracting officers lack incentives to depart from the FAR.

Conclusions

Based upon my personal experience in outsourcing both as a contractor and a government official employing contractors and the current research, several common themes or issues emerge. These are aligned with the framework for analysis employed in this book, which goes beyond accountability, the privileged domain of the GAO.

The FAR and OTAs

I cannot help noting the following: Secretary of Defense Gates avoided the FAR in obtaining mine-resistant, ambush-protected vehicles; Secretary of Defense Carter, who terms himself "acquisition czar," has no reference to the FAR in the index of his book; the Commission on Wartime Contracting in Iraq and Afghanistan found that the FAR was not followed in contingency operations; the IC did not adhere to the FAR in creating In-Q-Tel, nor did Carter adhere to it in creating the DIU; and the mere fact of utilization of OTAs signifies that the FAR is not always adhered to, even though some OTAs include elements of the FAR. These instances could be considered evidence that the FAR, for which I use the analogy of what is learned in a Yeshiva, is so extensive and so proscriptive that it encourages a culture of risk avoidance among COs. One of my informants observed: "The FAR spells out what you can do, and all the rest is not possible to do."[1] These observations, combined with the risk-avoidance culture of COs noted in the thorough, heavily empirical, and interview-based Lopes dissertation, the 2020 RAND report, and the Soloway and colleagues report, suggest that either the FAR must be simplified, or the culture must be modified, or both. I believe the evidence is clear that if another acquisition framework—OTAs—is required to obtain new technology, there must be other lost opportunities, in innovation and funding, by stolid adherence to the massive FAR. One must of course be sensitive to the incentives, or lack of same, for the COs. In following the FAR, COs do not run a risk. Having suffered multiple visits of US Navy inspector general investigations and observed the arbitrary nature of punishments in DoD and the armed services, one can appreciate, if not condone, the risk avoidance of COs. The result is, however, that the incentives of the COs in adhering to the FAR run counter to the goal of the effort by Congress, DoD, and the armed services to acquire new technologies from nontraditional contractors, which follows from the national defense strategy of 2018.

Oversight

Based on my own experience during more than twenty-five years as an employee of DoD and the research for this book, I do not expect significant improvements from DoD. As Secretary of Defense Carter states: "The Secretary of Defense is in charge of the largest and most complex organization in the entire world."[2] The bureaucratic inertia is simply too great. Nor is it likely that the industry will be supportive of major changes; it has its proven approach to things, employs lots of people, and makes a profit. The industry has at its beck and call legions of lawyers and lobbyists and oodles of retired DoD officials, both military and civilian.

It cannot be expected that such a huge bureaucracy can always get things right in contracting-out, especially, as Secretary of Defense Carter states, it awards 10 million contracts per year.[3] It is therefore important that Congress, which holds hearings, has the services of the CRS and GAO, and can create institutions such as the Commission on Wartime Contracting in Iraq and Afghanistan, SIGIR, and SIGAR that keep track of what is being done, or not, by DoD. The authorities of Congress are extensive and are made real by their control of the purse. The interest of Congress in the issues dealt with in this book is obvious by reading the NDAAs, which for fiscal year 2022 is the sixty-first NDAA. This NDAA specifically notes the analysis of GAO, "Contingency Contracting: DOD Has Taken Steps," and states that "we direct the Secretary of Defense to implement the recommendations of the GAO report and provide a progress briefing to the congressional defense committees not later than July 1, 2022."[4] It appears its success in dealing with outsourcing for personnel in the IC for the global war on terrorism may be repeated in the area of contingency contracting.

Indicative of its heightened interest in acquisitions, Congress in the fiscal year 2020 [10 US Code 2361a(a)] NDAA, directed DoD to create a multi-university consortium, the Acquisition Innovation Research Center, whose purpose is "to infuse innovation and alternative methods needed to better respond to the rapid increase of technological advancements critical to today's warfighter."[5]

Education and Training

There is extensive training, or maybe a better term is indoctrination, for COs in the FAR. However, even if OTAs are to remain a small percentage of what DoD outsources, considering the flexibility of OTAs and the large role of the agreement officer, there must be education/training for these agreement officers. This was stipulated in the 2018 NDAA, but as far as I can ascertain through due diligence, there is minimal education/training. Further, and in line with the next category, it seems likely that the United States will engage in future contingency operations. It is therefore essential that non-acquisition military officers receive education/training in dealing with contractors. This was stipulated in Section 849 in the NDAA for fiscal year 2008, but never implemented. In both cases, education and training in the use of OTAs by COs, and education and training on the care and feeding of contractors for military commanders, necessitate attention to incentives or, more accurately, disincentives for both.

Strategy

As Lewis Carroll wrote in *Alice's Adventures in Wonderland:* "If you don't know where you're going, any road will get you there." This observation summarizes the significance of the lack of strategy in the global war on terrorism. According to Special Inspector General for Afghanistan John F. Sopko's final report, despite the fiascos in Afghanistan and Iraq, there is a possibility that the United States will pursue contingency contracting elsewhere.[6] If so, I imagine that North Africa is the most likely venue. Hopefully, the guidance in the fiscal year 2022 NDAA to DoD to report back on the reforms made to contingency contracting recommended by the Commission on Wartime Contracting in Iraq and Afghanistan will be implemented and the fiascos of Iraq and Afghanistan will be avoided in the future.

Implementation

All the available literature, reflective of my personal experience with junior officers at the Naval Postgraduate School who had been CORs in Iraq and Afghanistan, concludes that the COR function, as collateral duty for junior officers, simply does not work. This function should be eliminated and the officers in charge of operations should fulfill this role.[7] Currently, while there have been proposals, there are no institutions for implementation of OTAs. Rather, Congress itself receives information on OTAs, through hearings, the GAO, and the CRS. Only if OTAs catch on more than they have so far may it become necessary to create one or more institutions to see to implementation.

Resources

According to the CRS, in fiscal year 2020, when DoD contracted out $420 billion, 51 percent of the total was for services, 41 percent for goods, and 8 percent for research and development.[8] As noted in the introduction to this book, there is no single definition of what constitutes a service for DoD, and not surprisingly the data are inconsistent. What is clear, however, is that the percentage of funds contracted out for services continues to exceed that contracted out for goods. There are two major considerations of relevance for outsourcing for services. First, according to the GAO, it has highlighted services as an issue in its classification of DoD outsourcing as high-risk since 1991.[9] Second, it is common knowledge that it is much more difficult for COs to award and supervise contracts for services than it is for things. This is clear in the literature, and it has been pointed out to me in an interview by an expert, professionally and academically, in contracting.

Final Thoughts

The theme of innovation pervades the rhetoric of acquisitions in DoD with the creation of the Army Futures Command, the Defense Innovation Unit, and the Strategic Capabilities Office, all with "a mandate to improve DoD's adoption of advanced technologies and accelerate its pace of innovation."[10] However, the analysis and recommendations of the Packard Commission report could just as easily be done today as in 1986, and Michael Brown, director of the DIU, did not extend his directorship, although he could have, alleging that DoD is not moving fast enough in incorporating commercially available technologies into the acquisition process. The lack of urgency for DoD to innovate is captured in the title of an article written by a highly regarded professional, who has experience as a staffer on the Senate Armed Services Committee and as deputy defense secretary for industrial policy, Bill Greenwalt: "DIU's Director Tried to Overcome a Calcified Defense Innovation System. It Beat Him, Now What?"[11] He raises the possibility that, under President Xi Jinping, China stifles innovation by relying on the Communist bureaucracy so the United States won't fall so far behind in technological innovation. Also, as reported in Chapter 2 on fact versus rhetoric on innovation, the email message from the main expert on the issue of acquisitions at the Congressional Research Service is telling. She wrote: "DOD tends to throw around the word 'innovation' frequently, and not always in reference to a genuinely innovative capability. Sometimes, 'innovation' to DOD is nothing more than rearranging the deck chairs."[12] My greatest hope for change lies in the newly created Acquisition Innovation Research Center. This book is, amazingly enough, the first book that deals with acquisition authorities from a social science perspective. I hope it will stimulate other social scientists, as well as acquisition professionals in the AIRC, to research and publish on this topic. The AIRC was created by Congress to "infuse innovation and alternative methods in acquisitions." And, composed of units in prestigious universities specializing in acquisitions rather than "the industry," DoD, or DoD "schoolhouses," it should have both the independence and the competence to make these recommendations.[13]

Notes

1. Official at the NPS in the Emerging Technology Consortium.
2. Ash Carter, *Inside the Five-Sided Box: Lessons from a Lifetime of Leadership in the Pentagon* (New York: Dutton, 2019), p. 3.

3. Ibid., p. 9.

4. Page 210 of 670 of "Joint Explanatory Statement for the NDAA for FY 2020."

5. Available at https://acqirc.org/about.

6. John F. Sopko, "What We Need to Learn: Lessons from Twenty Years of Afghanistan Reconstruction" (Washington, DC, August 2021), p. xiii.

7. While somewhat different from training/education for dealing with contractors in contingency operations, it appears that DoD has several problems with training. See GAO, "Defense Workforce: Steps Needed to Identify Acquisition Training Needs for Non-Acquisition Personnel" (Washington, DC, September 2019).

8. *CRS In Focus,* "Department of Defense Contractors" (Washington, DC, December 17, 2021).

9. GAO, "Service Acquisitions: DOD's Report to Congress Identifies Steps Taken to Improve Management, but Does Not Address Some Key Planning Issues" (Washington, DC, February 22, 2021), "Fast Facts."

10. Nathan Voss and James Ryseff, *Comparing the Organizational Cultures of the Department of Defense and Silicon Valley* (Santa Monica: RAND, 2022), p. 38.

11. https://www.aei.org/op-eds/dius-director-tried-to-overcome-a-calcified-defense-innovation-system-it-beat-him-now-what/.

12. Email from CRS expert on November 6, 2020. Staff of Congress, including the CRS, must remain anonymous.

13. To ensure the work of the AIRC is most useful, Congress should mandate the GAO to conduct a study of the degree of implementation of the mandates in the NDAA for FY 2018 regarding the "preference for" using OTAs and education and training in their use.

Acronyms

AAF	Adaptive Acquisition Framework
AEF	American Expeditionary Forces
AFRICOM	Africa Command
AI	artificial intelligence
CENTCOM	Central Command
CIA	Central Intelligence Agency
CICA	Competition in Contracting Act
CMMC	Cybersecurity Maturity Model Certification
CNAS	Center for a New American Security
CO	contracting officer
COR	contracting officer representative
COSSI	Commercial Operations and Support Savings Initiative
CRS	Congressional Research Service
CSIS	Center for Security and International Studies
DARPA	Defense Advanced Research Projects Agency
DFARS	Defense Federal Acquisition Regulation Supplement
DIU	Defense Innovation Unit
DNI	director of national intelligence
DoD	Department of Defense
ETC	Emerging Technology Consortium
FAR	Federal Acquisition Regulation
FBI	Federal Bureau of Investigation

FPDS	Federal Procurement Data System
GAO	Government Accountability Office
IC	intelligence community
IDIQ	indefinite-delivery/indefinite-quantity
IT	information technology
LOGCAP	Logistics Civil Augmentation Program
NASA	National Aeronautics and Space Administration
NATO	North Atlantic Treaty Organization
NDAA	National Defense Authorization Act
NGO	nongovernmental organization
NIS	national intelligence strategy
NPS	Naval Postgraduate School
NSC	National Security Council
NSIC	National Security Innovation Capital
NSIN	National Security Innovation Network
NSS	national security strategy
OCS	operational contract support
ODNI	Office of the Director of National Intelligence
OMB	Office of Management and Budget
OTA	Other Transaction Authority
PPE	personal protective equipment
PSC	private security contractor
R&D	research and development
SIGAR	special inspector general for Afghan reconstruction
SIGIR	special inspector general for Iraq reconstruction
USAID	US Agency for International Development

Bibliography

Adams, Gordon. *Controlling Weapons Costs: Can the Pentagon's Reforms Work?* New York: Council on Economic Priorities, 1983.

Adams, Gordon. *The Politics of Defense Contracting: The Iron Triangle.* New Brunswick: Transaction, 1982.

Almonte, Alison D. "Analysis of Nontraditional Contractors as a Proxy for Innovation Through DOD Other Transaction Agreements." Master's thesis. December 2019. http://www.nps.edu/library.

American Bar Association. *Government Contract Law: The Deskbook for Procurement Professionals.* 3rd ed. Chicago, 2007.

Atkinson, Robert D. "Understanding the U.S. National Innovation System, 2020." Washington, DC: Information Technology & Innovation Foundation, November 2020.

Avant, Deborah. *Political Institutions and Military Change: Lessons from Peripheral Wars.* Ithaca: Cornell University Press, 1994.

Barnard, Chester. *The Functions of the Executive.* Cambridge: Harvard University Press, 1962 (originally published 1938).

Barnes, Julian A. "C.I.A. Chief Is Reorganizing Agency to Focus on Challenges from China." *New York Times,* October 2, 2021.

Batka, Caroline, Molly Dunigan, and Rachel Burns. "Private Military Contractors' Financial Experiences and Incentives. *Defense & Security Analysis* 36, no. 2 (2020): 161–179.

Bensahel, Nora. "Mission Not Accomplished: What Went Wrong with Iraqi Reconstruction." *Journal of Strategic Studies* 29, no. 3 (June 2006): 453–473.

Bensahel, Nora, Olga Oliker, Keith Crane, Richard R. Brennan Jr., Heather S. Gregg, Thomas Sullivan, and Andrew Rathmel. *After Saddam: Prewar Planning and the Occupation of Iraq.* Santa Monica: RAND Arroyo Center, 2008.

Bibliography

Bovens, Mark. "Analysing and Assessing Public Accountability: A Conceptual Framework." European Governance Papers (EUROGOV) n. C-06-01, 2006. http://www.connex-network.org/eurogov/pdf/egp-connex-C-06-01.pdf.

Bresler, Amanda, and Alex Bresler. "Analyzing the Composition of the Department of Defense Small Business Industrial Base." 2021. https://media-exp1.licdn.com/dms/document/C4D1FAQEOxhFMS9MKRg/feedshare-document-pdf-analyzed/0/1650309424054?e=2147483647&v=beta&t=nryjkSKhaiXj-VvGUXgZhnFSCT4XonrsZ6QHHJyHT4c.

Brose, Christian. *The Kill Chain: Defending America in the Future of High-Tech Warfare.* New York: Hachette, 2020.

Brown, Shannon. *Providing the Means of War: Historical Perspectives on Defense Acquisition, 1945–2000.* Washington, DC: US Army Center of Military History and Industrial College of the Armed Forces, 2005.

Bruneau, Thomas C. "Contracting Out Security." *Journal of Strategic Studies* 36, no. 5 (October 2013): 638–665.

———. "Effectiveness in Comparative Perspective." In Carlos Solar, ed., *The Armed Forces and Democracy: Governing the Military in Chile.* Manchester: Manchester University Press, 2022.

———. "Impediments to Fighting the Islamic State: Private Contractors and US Strategy." *Journal of Strategic Studies* 39, no. 1 (February 2016): 120–141.

———. *Patriots for Profit: Contractors and the Military in U.S. National Security.* Stanford: Stanford University Press, 2011.

———. "Requirements for Military Effectiveness: Chile in Comparative Perspective." Washington, DC: William J. Perry Center for Hemispheric Defense Studies, March 2020.

Bruneau, Thomas C., and Steven C. Boraz, eds. *Reforming Intelligence: Obstacles to Democratic Control and Effectiveness.* Austin: University of Texas Press, 2007.

Bruneau, Thomas C., and Aurel Croissant, eds. *Civil-Military Relations: Control and Effectiveness Across Regimes.* Boulder: Lynne Rienner, 2019.

Bruneau, Thomas C., and Richard B. Goetze. "From Tragedy to Success in Colombia: The Centrality of Effectiveness in Civil-Military Relations." In Florina Cristiana Matei, Carolyn Halladay, and Thomas Bruneau, eds., *The Routledge Handbook of Civil-Military Relations,* 2nd ed. London: Routledge, 2021.

Bruneau, Thomas C., and Florina Cristiana Matei. "Brazil: The Ebb and Flow of Democratic Civilian Control." In Florina Cristiana Matei, Carolyn Halladay, and Thomas Bruneau, eds., *The Routledge Handbook of Civil-Military Relations,* 2nd ed. London: Routledge, 2021.

Bruneau, Thomas C., and Scott D. Tollefson, eds. *Who Guards the Guardians, and How Democratic Civil-Military Relations.* Austin: University of Texas Press, 2006.

Bibliography

Cancian, Mark F. "U.S. Military Forces in FY 2020." Washington, DC: Center for Strategic and International Studies, October 2019.

———. "U.S. Military Forces in FY 2022." Washington, DC: Center for Strategic and International Studies, October 2021.

Carter, Ash. *Inside the Five-Sided Box: Lessons from a Lifetime of Leadership in the Pentagon.* New York: Dutton, 2019.

Cecire, Michael H. "Covid-19 and Domestic PPE Production and Distribution: Issues and Policy Options." Washington, DC: Congressional Research Service, December 7, 2020.

Center for Government Contracting, George Mason University. "Other Transactions Authority: A Unique Perspective from Government, Industry, and Academia." Fairfax, VA, December 9, 2021. Podcast. https://business.gmu.edu/govcon/webinars-podcasts-and-virtual-networking-events.

Center for Strategic and International Studies (CSIS). "Connecting the U.S. Innovation Ecosystem with National Security." Washington, DC, September 23, 2021. Podcast. https://www.csis.org/events/connecting-us-innovation-ecosystem-national-security.

———. "Maintaining the Intelligence Edge: Reimagining and Reinventing Intelligence Through Innovation." Washington, DC, January 2021.

Chesterman, Simon. "'We Can't Spy . . . If We Can't Buy': The Privatization of Intelligence and the Limits of Outsourcing 'Inherently Governmental Functions.'" *European Journal of International Law* 19, no. 5 (2008): 1055–1074.

Chesterman, Simon, and Angelina Fisher, eds. *Private Security, Public Order: The Out-Sourcing of Public Services and Its Limits.* New York: Oxford University Press, 2009.

Chesterman, Simon, and Chia Lehnardt, eds. *From Mercenaries to Market: The Rise and Regulation of Private Security Companies.* New York: Oxford University Press, 2007.

Christensen, Thomas J. *The China Challenge: Shaping the Choices of a Rising Power.* New York: Norton, 2015.

Collins, Joseph J. "Choosing War: The Decision to Invade Iraq and Its Aftermath." Washington, DC: Institute for National Strategic Studies, National Defense University, April 2008.

Commission on Army Acquisition and Program Management in Expeditionary Operations (Gansler Commission). "Urgent Reform Required: Army Expeditionary Contracting." Washington, DC: October 31, 2007.

Commission on Wartime Contracting in Iraq and Afghanistan. "Transforming Wartime Contracting: Controlling Costs, Reducing Risks—Final Report to Congress." Washington, DC: August 29, 2011.

Cordesman, Anthony F. "The Reasons for the Collapse of Afghan Forces." Washington, DC: Center for Strategic and International Studies, August 17, 2021.

Bibliography

CRS In Focus. "A-76 Competitions in the Department of Defense." Washington, DC, June 2, 2020.

———. "Defense Primer: Department of Defense Contractors." Washington, DC, December 17, 2021.

———. "The Director of National Intelligence (DNI)." Washington, DC, June 7, 2021.

———. "Emerging Military Technologies: Background and Issues for Congress." Washington, DC, December 21, 2021.

———. "Evaluating DOD Strategy: Key Findings of the National Defense Strategy Commission." Washington, DC, March 19, 2019.

———. "FY 2022 NDAA: Strategic Context." Washington, DC, November 3, 2021.

———. "The Interim National Security Strategic Guidance." Washington, DC, March 29, 2021.

———. "National and Defense Intelligence." Washington, DC, December 30, 2020.

———. "Regular Military Compensation." Washington, DC, December 26, 2019.

———. "Under Secretary of Defense for Intelligence and Security." Washington, DC, December 30, 2020.

CRS Insight. "FY2022 NDAA: Research, Development, Test and Evaluation Authorizations." Washington, DC, March 18, 2022.

Dahl, Erik J. "Why Won't They Listen? Comparing Receptivity Toward Intelligence at Pearl Harbor and Midway." *Intelligence and National Security* 28, no. 1 (2013): 68–90.

Davis, Christopher M., et al. "Congressional Oversight Manual." Washington, DC: Congressional Research Service, March 31, 2021.

Deltec. "The Ins & Outs of Other Transaction Agreements (OTAs)." September 17, 2020. Webinar presented by BDO USA.

DeVine, Michael E. "Congressional Oversight of Intelligence: Background and Selected Options for Further Reform." Washington, DC: Congressional Research Service, December 4, 2018.

———. "Intelligence Community Spending: Trends and Issues." Washington, DC: Congressional Research Service, June 18, 2018.

Dew, Nicholas, and Bryan Hudgens. "The Evolving Private Military Sector: A Survey." Monterey, CA: Naval Postgraduate School, Acquisition Research Program, Graduate School of Business and Public Policy. http://www.acquisitionsresearch.org.

Donahue, John D. *The Privatization Decision: Public Ends, Private Means.* New York: Basic, 1989.

Dunigan, Molly. *Victory for Hire; Private Security Contractors' Impact on Military Effectiveness.* Stanford: Stanford University Press, 2011.

Dunigan, Molly, et al. "Human Capital Needs for the Department of Defense Operational Contract Support: Planning and Integration Workforce." Santa Monica: RAND, 2017.

Dunn, Richard L. "Injecting New Ideas and New Approaches in Defense Systems: Are 'Other Transactions' an Answer?" May 2009. https://nps.edu/web/acqnresearch/dair.

———. "2021 NDAA: All Systems GO for Other Transactions! But Curiosity About So-Called 'Consortia.'" Florida: Strategic Institute FOR Innovation in Government Contracting, January 28, 2021. https://strategicinstitute.org.

Ellis, James O., James N. Mattis, and Kori Schake. "Restoring Our National Security." In George P. Shultz, ed., *Blueprint for America*. Stanford: Hoover Institution Press, 2016.

Elsea, Jennifer K., et al. "Private Security Contractors in Iraq: Legal Issues." Washington, DC: Congressional Research Service, September 29, 2008.

Federal Acquisition Regulation. https://www.acquisition.gov/browse/index/far.

Fontaine, Richard, and John Nagl. "Contracting in Conflicts: The Path to Reform." Washington, DC: Center for a New American Security, June 2010.

Fox, J. Ronald. *Arming America: How the U.S. Buys Weapons*. Boston: Harvard University Press, 1974.

———. *Defense Acquisition Reform, 1960–2009: An Elusive Goal*. Washington, DC: US Army Center of Military History, 2021.

Gaddis, John Lewis. *On Grand Strategy*. New York: Penguin, 2019.

Gansler, Jacques S. "Acquisition Reform: Achieving 21st Century National Security." Testimony before the Senate Armed Services Committee, March 3, 2009.

Gates, Robert M. *Duty: Memoirs of a Secretary at War*. New York: Knopf, 2014.

Gilli, Andrea, and Mauro Gilli. "Why China Has Not Caught Up Yet." *International Security* 43, no. 3 (Winter 2018): 141–189.

Government Accountability Office (GAO). "Afghanistan Reconstruction: GAO Work Since 2002 Shows Systemic Internal Control Weaknesses That Increased the Risk of Waste, Fraud, and Abuse." Washington, DC: Government Accountability Office, January 27, 2021. GAO-21-32R.

———. "Army Should Improve Use of Alternative Agreements and Approaches by Enhancing Oversight and Communication of Lessons Learned." Washington, DC: Government Accountability Office, October 2020. GAO-21-8.

———. "Civilian Intelligence Community: Additional Actions Needed to Improve Reporting on and Planning for the Use of Contract Personnel." Washington, DC, January 2014. GAO-14-204.

———. "Civilian Intelligence Community: Additional Actions Needed to Improve Reporting on and Planning for the Use of Contract Personnel." Washington, DC, February 13, 2014. GAO-14-257T.

———. "Contingency Contracting: Agency Actions to Address Recommendations by the Commission on Wartime Contracting in Iraq and Afghanistan." Washington, DC, August 1, 2012. GAO-12-854R.

———. "Contingency Contracting: DOD Has Taken Steps to Address Commission Recommendations, but Should Better Document Progress and Improve Contract Data." Washington, DC, September 2021. GAO-21-344.

———. "Covid-19 Contracting: Actions Needed to Enhance Transparency and Oversight of Selected Awards." Washington, DC, July 2021. GAO-21-501.

———. "Covid-19 Contracting: Observations on Federal Contracting in Response to the Pandemic." Washington, DC, July 2020. GAO-20-632.

———. "Defense Acquisition: Addressing Incentives Is Key to Further Reform Efforts." Testimony before the Senate Committee on Armed Services, April 30, 2014. GAO-14-563T.

———. "Defense Acquisitions Annual Assessment: Drive to Deliver Capabilities Faster Increases Importance of Program Knowledge and Consistent Data for Oversight." Washington, DC, June 2020. GAO-20-439.

———. "Defense Contracting: Improved Policies and Tools Could Help Increase Competition on DOD's National Security Exception Procurements." Washington, DC, January 2012. GAO-12-263.

———. "Defense Logistics: High-Level DOD Coordination Is Needed to Further Improve the Management of the Army's LOGCAP Contract." Washington, DC, March 2005. GAO-05-328.

———. "Defense Workforce: Steps Needed to Identify Acquisition Training Needs for Non-Acquisition Personnel." Washington, DC, September 2019. GAO-19-556.

———. "DOD Fraud Risk Management: Actions Needed to Enhance Department-Wide Approach, Focusing on Procurement Fraud Risks." Washington, DC, August 2021. GAO-21-309.

———. "DOD's Use of Other Transactions for Prototype Projects Has Increased." Washington, DC, November 2019. GAO-20-84.

———. "Federal Acquisitions: Use of 'Other Transaction' Agreements Limited and Mostly for Research and Development Activities." Washington, DC, January 7, 2016. GAO 16-209.

———. "Federal Contracting: Senior Leaders Should Use Leading Companies' Key Practices to Improve Performance." Washington, DC: Government Accountability Office, July 2021. GAO-21-491.

———. "High-Risk Series: Dedicated Leadership Needed to Address Limited Progress in Most High-Risk Areas." Washington, DC, March 2021. GAO-21-119SP.

———. "Intelligence Community: Actions Need to Improve Planning and Oversight of the Center for Academic Excellence Program." Washington, DC, August 1, 2019. GAO-19-529.

———. "Military Acquisitions: DOD Is Taking Steps to Address Challenges Faced by Certain Companies." Washington, DC, July 2017. GAO-17-644.

———. "Military Operations: Contractors Provide Vital Services to Deployed Forces but Are Not Adequately Addressed in DOD Plans." Washington, DC, June 24, 2003. GAO-03-695.

———. "Military Readiness: Department of Defense Domain Readiness Varied from Fiscal Year 2017 Through Fiscal Year 2019." Washington, DC, April 2021. GAO-21-279.

———. "Operational Contract Support: Additional Actions Needed to Manage, Account for, and Vet Defense Contractors in Africa." Washington, DC, December 17, 2015. GAO-16-105.

———. "Private Security Contractors: DOD Needs to Better Identify and Monitor Personnel and Contracts." Washington, DC, July 2021. GAO-21-255.

———. "Report to Congressional Committees. Cybersecurity: DOD Needs to Take Decisive Actions to Improve Cyber Hygiene." Washington, DC, April 2020. GAO-20-241.

———. "Report to Congressional Committees. Defense Contractors: Information on the Impact of Reducing the Cap on Employee Compensation Costs." Washington, DC, June 2013. GAO-13-566.

———. "Report to Congressional Requesters: Cybersecurity: Clarity of Leadership Urgently Needed to Fully Implement the National Strategy." Washington, DC, September 2020. GAO-20-629.

———. "Service Acquisitions: DOD's Report to Congress Identifies Steps Taken to Improve Management, but Does Not Address Some Key Planning Issues." Washington, DC, February 22, 2021. GAO-21-267R.

———. "Warfighter Support: Continued Actions Needed by DOD to Improve and Institutionalize Contractor Support in Contingency Operations." Washington, DC, March 17, 2010. GAO-10-551T.

———. "Warfighter Support: DOD Needs Additional Steps to Fully Integrate Operational Contract Support into Contingency Planning." Washington, DC, February 8, 2013. GAO-13-212.

GovWin IQ. "Other Transaction Agreements (OTAs)." Arlington, VA: Deltec, February 10, 2021.

Griffith, Erin. "Holmes Caps Her Defense with Round of Denials." *New York Times,* December 8, 2021.

Grimmett, Richard F., coordinator. "9/11 Commission Recommendations: Implementation Status." Washington, DC: Congressional Research Service, December 4, 2006.

Haass, Richard N. *War of Necessity, War of Choice: A Memoir of Two Iraq Wars.* New York: Simon and Schuster, 2009.

Halchin, Elaine L. "Circular A-76 Revision 2003: Selected Issues." Washington, DC: Congressional Research Service, January 7, 2005.

———. "The Intelligence Community and Its Use of Contractors: Congressional Oversight Issues." Washington, DC: Congressional Research Service, August 18, 2015.

Hansen, Morten. "Intelligence Contracting: On the Motivations, Interests, and Capabilities of Core Personnel Contractors in the US Intelligence Community." *Intelligence and National Security* 29, no. 1 (2014): 58–81.

Harman, Jane. "Preface: Why Intelligence Oversight Matters." In Zachary K. Goldman and Samuel J. Rascoff, eds., *Global Intelligence Oversight: Governing Security in the Twenty-First Century.* New York: Oxford University Press, 2016.

Hicks, Kathleen H., and Andrew Hunter. "Assessing the Third Offset Strategy." Washington, DC: Center for Strategic and International Studies, March 2017.

Johnson, Loch K. *National Security Intelligence: Secret Operations in Defense of the Democracies.* 2nd ed. Cambridge: Polity, 2017.

Joyce, Renanah Miles, and Brian Blankenship. "'Money as a Weapon System': The Promises and Pitfalls of Foreign Defense Contracting." Washington, DC: Cato Institute, June 3, 2020.

Kendall, Frank. "Cybersecurity Maturity Model Certification: An Idea Whose Time Has Not Come and Never May." *Forbes,* April 29, 2020.

Kidwell, Deborah. *Private War, Public Fight? The United States and Private Military Companies.* Lulu.com, 2011.

Kinsey, Christopher. *Corporate Soldiers and International Security: The Rise of Private Military Companies.* London: Routledge, 2006.

Kitts, Kenneth. *Presidential Commissions and National Security: The Politics of Damage Control.* Boulder: Lynne Rienner, 2006.

Kosar, Kevin. "Privatization and the Federal Government: An Introduction." Washington, DC: Congressional Research Service, December 28, 2006.

Laffont, Jean-Jacques, and David Martifort. *The Theory of Incentives I: The Principal-Agent Model.* Princeton: Princeton University Press, 2002.

Lazear, Edward P. "Compensation and Incentives in the Workplace." *Journal of Economic Perspectives* 32, no. 3 (Summer 2018): 195–214.

Leander, Anna. *Eroding State Authority? Private Military Companies and the Legitimate Use of Force.* Rome: Rubbettino Editore, 2006.

LeDoux, Karen E. "LOGCAP 101: An Operational Planner's Guide." *Army Logistician* (May–June 2005): 24–29.

Lewis, James Andrew. "National Security and the Innovation Ecosystem." Washington, DC: Center for Strategic and International Studies, October 2021.

Liang, Colonel Quao, and Colonel Wang Xiangsui. *Un-Restricted Warfare.* Brattleboro, VT: Echo Point Books and Media, 1999.

Light, Paul C. *A Government Ill Executed: The Decline of the Federal Service and How to Reverse It.* Cambridge: Harvard University Press, 2008.

———. *The True Size of Government.* Washington, DC: Brookings Institution, 1999.

Lopes, Crane. "Historical Institutionalism and Defense Public Procurement: The Case of Other Transactions Agreements." Dissertation. September 19, 2018.

Lowenthal, Mark M. *Intelligence: From Secrets to Policy.* 8th ed. Thousand Oaks, CA: Sage, 2020.

Luckey, John R. "Explanation and Discussion of the Recently Revised Federal Outsourcing Policy." OMB Circular no. A-76. Washington, DC: Congressional Research Service, September 10, 2003.

Manuel, Kate M. "Definitions of 'Inherently Governmental Function' in Federal Procurement Law and Guidance." Washington, DC: Congressional Research Service, December 23, 2014.

Manuel, Kate M., et al. "The Federal Acquisition Regulation (FAR): Answers to Frequently Asked Questions." Washington, DC: Congressional Research Service, February 3, 2015.

Mayer, Lauren A., et al. "Prototyping Using Other Transactions: Case Studies for the Acquisition Community." Santa Monica: RAND, 2020.

Mazarr, Michael J. "Understanding Competition: Great Power Rivalry in a Changing International Order—Concepts and Theories." Santa Monica: RAND, March 2022.

McBride, James, and Andrew Chatzky. "Is 'Made in China 2025' a Threat to Global Trade?" Washington, DC: Council on Foreign Relations, May 13, 2019.

McCormick, Rhys. "Defense Acquisition Trends 2020: Topline DoD Trends." Washington, DC: Center for Strategic and International Studies, October 2020.

———. "Department of Defense Other Transaction Authority Trends: A New R&D Funding Paradigm?" Washington, DC: Center for Strategic and International Studies, December 2020.

McCormick, Rhys, and Gregory Sanders. *Trends in Department of Defense Other Transaction Authority Usage.* Lanham: Rowman and Littlefield, May 2022.

McDonnell, Janet. "A History of Defense Contract Administration." March 5, 2020. https://www.dcma.mil/News/Article-View/Article/2100501/a-history-of-defense-contract-administration/.

McFate, Sean. "America's Addiction to Mercenaries." *The Atlantic*, August 2, 2016.

———. *The Modern Mercenary: Private Armies and What They Mean for World Order*. London: Oxford University Press, 2015.

Medeiros, Evan S., and Jude Blanchette. "Beyond Colossus or Collapse: Five Myths Driving American Debates About China." *War on the Rocks*, March 19, 2021.

Mendel, Robert. *The Privatization of Security*. Boulder: Lynne Rienner, 2002.

Merritt, Geoff, and Shohei Takagi. "The Ins & Outs of Other Transaction Agreements (OTAs)." Arlington, VA: BDO for Deltec, webinar, September 17, 2020.

Michaels, Jon D. "The (Willingly) Fettered Executive: Presidential Spinoffs in National Security Domains and Beyond." *Virginia Law Review* 97, no. 4 (May 19, 2011): 801–898.

Miles, Anne Daugherty. "The U.S. Intelligence Community: Selected Cross-Cutting Issues." Washington, DC: Congressional Research Service, April 12, 2016.

Molzahn, Wendy. "The CIA's In-Q-Tel Model: Its Applicability." *Acquisition Review Quarterly* (Winter 2003): 47–61.

Nagle, James F. *A History of Government Contracting*. 2nd ed. Washington, DC: George Washington University Press, 2005.

Nakasone, Paul M., and Michael Sulmeyer. "How to Compete in Cyberspace: Cyber Command's New Approach." *Foreign Affairs* (September–October 2020): https://www.foreignaffairs.com/articles/united-states/2020-08-25/cybersecurity.

National Defense Strategy Commission. "Providing for the Common Defense: The Assessment and Recommendations of the National Defense Strategy Commission." Washington, DC, 2019.

Nemfakos, Charles, et al. "Workforce Planning in the Intelligence Community: A Retrospective." Santa Monica: RAND, 2013.

Olney, Rachel. "The Rift Between Silicon Valley and the Pentagon Is Economic, Not Moral." *War on the Rocks*, January 28, 2018.

O'Mara, Margaret. *The Code: Silicon Valley and the Remaking of America*. New York: Penguin, 2019.

O'Rourke, Ronald. "Renewed Great Power Competition: Implications for Defense—Issues for Congress." Washington, DC: Congressional Research Service, updated biannually.

Patch, B. W. "War Contracts and Profit Limitation." Editorial Research Report 1942, vol. 11. https://library.cqpress.com/cqresearcher/document.php?id=cqresrre1942110600.

Peters, Heidi M. "Defense Acquisitions: DOD's Cybersecurity Maturity Model Certification Framework." Washington, DC: Congressional Research Service, December 18, 2020.

———. "Department of Defense Contractor and Troop Levels in Afghanistan and Iraq: 2007–2020." Washington, DC: Congressional Research Service, February 22, 2021.

———. "Department of Defense Use of Other Transaction Authority: Background, Analysis, and Issues for Congress." Washington, DC: Congressional Research Service, February 22, 2019.

Pfaff, C. Anthony, and Edward Mienie. "Strategic Insights: Five Myths Associated with Employing Private Military Companies." Carlisle, PA: US Army War College, April 5, 2019.

"Piloting a Bipartisan Ship: Strategies and Tactics of the 9/11 Commission." Cambridge: Kennedy School of Government, 2005.

Pion-Berlin, David, Thomas Bruneau, and Richard B. Goetze Jr. "The Trump Self-Coup Attempt: Comparisons and Civil-Military Relations." *Government and Opposition* (2022): 1–18. https://doi.org/10.1017/gov.2022.13.

Priest, Dana, and William Arkin. *Top Secret America: The Rise of the New American Security State.* New York: Little, Brown, 2011.

Reinert, John T. "In-Q-Tel: The Central Intelligence Agency as Venture Capitalist." *Northwestern Journal of International Law & Business* 33 (Spring 2013): 677–709.

Rendon, Rene G., and Keith F. Snider, eds. *Management of Defense Acquisition Projects.* Palmdale, CA: Lockheed Martin Corporation for Institute of Aeronautics and Astronautics, 2008.

Ricks, Thomas. *Fiasco: The American Military Adventure in Iraq.* New York: Penguin, 2006.

Risch, Erna. *Quartermaster Support of the Army, A History of the Corps 1775–1939.* Washington, DC: US Army Center of Military History, 1989.

Rollins, John. "Osama bin Laden's Death: Implications and Considerations." Washington, DC: Congressional Research Service, May 5, 2011.

Sabin, Jacob D., and Mark K. Zakner. "Analysis of Expedited Defense Contracting Methods in the Acquisition of Emerging Technology." Monterey, CA: Naval Postgraduate School, December 2016.

Sadat, General Sami. "I Commanded Afghan Troops: This Year We Were Betrayed." *New York Times,* August 25, 2021.

Sanders, Gregory, Won Joon Jang, and Alexander Holderness. "Defense Acquisition Trends 2021." Washington, DC: Center for Security and International Studies, March 2022.

Sanger, David E. "Don't Call It a Cold War: U.S. Labors to Name China Rivalry." *New York Times,* October 18, 2021.

Sargent, John F. Jr., and Marcy Gallo. "The Global Research and Development Landscape and Implications for the Department of

Defense." Washington, DC: Congressional Research Service, June 28, 2021.

Sargent, John F. Jr., et al. "Defense Acquisitions: How and Where DOD Spends Its Contracting Dollars." Washington, DC: Congressional Research Service, July 2, 2018.

Sayler, Kelley M. "Emerging Military Technologies: Background and Issues for Congress." Washington, DC: Congressional Research Service, November 10, 2021.

Scahill, Jeremy. *Blackwater: The Rise of the World's Most Powerful Mercenary Army.* New York: Nation, 2007.

Schwartz, Benjamin, and Bill Greenwalt. "Other Transaction Authority and the Consortia-Based Acquisition Model: A Valuable Tool for Rapid Defense Innovation." Washington, DC: Chertoff Group, 2020.

Schwartz, Moshe. "Defense Acquisition Reform: Background, Analysis, and Issues for Congress." Washington, DC: Congressional Research Service, May 23, 2014.

———. "Department of Defense's Use of Contractors to Support Military Operations: Background, Analysis, and Issues for Congress." Washington, DC: Congressional Research Service, May 17, 2013.

———. "Training the Military to Manage Contractors During Expeditionary Operations: Overview and Options for Congress." Washington, DC: Congressional Research Service, December 17, 2008.

Schwartz, Moshe, and Stephanie Halcrow. "The Power of Many: Leveraging Consortia to Promote Innovation, Expand the Defense Industrial Base, and Accelerate Innovation." Fairfax County, VA: George Mason University Center for Government Contracting, July 18, 2022.

Schwartz, Moshe, and Heidi M. Peters. "Acquisition Reform in the FY2016-FY2018 National Defense Authorization Acts (NDAAs)." Washington, DC: Congressional Research Service, January 19, 2018.

Schwartz, Moshe, John F. Sargent Jr., and Christopher T. Mann. "Defense Acquisitions: How and Where DOD Spends Its Contracting Dollars." Washington, DC: Congressional Research Service, July 2, 2018.

Shorrock, Tim. "Five Corporations Now Dominate Our Privatized Intelligence Industry." *The Atlantic*, September 8, 2016.

Singer, Peter W. *Corporate Warriors: The Rise of the Privatized Military Industry.* Ithaca: Cornell University Press, 2003.

Smith, Jean Edward. *Bush.* New York: Simon and Schuster, 2016.

Soloway, Stan, Jason Knudson, and Vincent Wroble. "Other Transaction Authorities: After 60 Years, Hitting Their Stride or Hitting the Wall?" Washington, DC: IBM Center for the Business of Government, 2021.

Sopko, John F. "Letter to Commanding Generals of U.S. Army Sustainment Command and U.S. Army Contracting Command." September

12, 2014. https://www.sigar.mil/pdf/special%20projects/SIGAR-14-97-SP.pdf.
———. "What We Need to Learn: Lessons from Twenty Years of Afghanistan Reconstruction." Washington, DC, August 2021.
Special Inspector General for Iraq Reconstruction (SIGIR). "Learning from Iraq: A Final Report of the Special Inspector General for Iraq Reconstruction." Washington, DC, March 2013.
———. "Need to Enhance Oversight of Theater-Wide Internal Security Services Contracts." Washington, DC, April 2009.
Stanberry, Scott A. *Federal Contracting Made Easy*. 4th ed. Tysons Corner, VA: Management Concepts, 2013.
Stanger, Allison. *One Nation Under Contract: The Outsourcing of American Power and the Future of Foreign Policy*. New Haven: Yale University Press, 2009.
Steinberg, Douglas. "Leveraging the Department of Defense's Other Transaction Authority to Foster a Twenty-First-Century Acquisition Ecosystem." *Public Contract Law Journal* 49, no. 3 (Spring 2020): 538–565.
Strachan, Hew. *The Direction of War: Contemporary Strategy in Historical Perspective*. Cambridge: Cambridge University Press, 2013.
Strategic Institute FOR Innovation in Government Contracting. *Guide to Other Transactions Authority*. 3rd ed. 2021. https://strategicinstitute.org.
Theohary, Catherine A., and John W. Rollins. "Cyberwarfare and Cyberterrorism: In Brief." Washington, DC: Congressional Research Service, March 27, 2015.
US Congress. "Acquisition Workforce: DOD Can Improve Its Management and Oversight by Tracking Data on Contractor Personnel and Taking Additional Actions." Testimony by John K. Needham before the Oversight and Investigations Subcommittee of the House Committee on Armed Services, April 28, 2009.
———. "Are We Striking the Right Balance?" Hearing before the Oversight of Government Management, the Federal Workforce, and the District of Colombia Subcommittee of the Senate Committee on Homeland Security and Governmental Affairs, September 20, 2011.
———. "DOD Needs to Reexamine Its Extensive Reliance on Contractors and Continue to Improve Management and Oversight." Testimony by David M. Walker before the Subcommittee on Readiness of the House Committee on Armed Services, March 11, 2008.
———. "The Intelligence Community: Keeping Watch Over Its Contractor Workforce." Hearing before the Senate Committee on Homeland Security and Governmental Affairs, June 18, 2014.

———. "Other Transaction Authority: Flexibility at the Expense of Accountability?" Hearing before the Subcommittee on Emerging Threats, Cybersecurity, and Science and Technology of the House Committee on Homeland Security, February 7, 2008.

———. "Rightly Scaled, Carefully Open, Infinitely Agile: Reconfiguring to Win the Innovation Race in the Intelligence Community." Washington, DC, 2020. https://intelligence.house.gov/uploadedfiles/final_start_report_v4.pdf.

US Department of Defense. "Applications of Quantum Technologies: Executive Summary." Washington, DC, October 2019.

———. "Contingency Contracting: A Framework for Reform, 2015 Update." Washington, DC, March 31, 2015.

———. "Contractor Support of U.S. Operations in the USCENTCOM Area of Responsibility," Washington, DC, April 2019.

———. "Emerging Capability and Prototyping." Version 1.0. Washington, DC, December 6, 2018.

———. "Memorandum: Taxonomy for the Acquisition of Services and Supplies & Equipment." Washington, DC, August 27, 2012.

———. "Other Transactions Guide." Version 1.0. Washington, DC, November 2018.

———. "Performance of the Defense Acquisition System: 2014 Annual Report." Washington, DC, June 13, 2014.

———. "Report of the Defense Science Board Task Force on Fulfillment of Urgent Operational Needs." Washington, DC, July 2009.

———. "Selected Manpower Statistics Fiscal Year 1990." Washington, DC, January 1, 1990.

———. "State of Competition Within the Defense Industrial Base." Washington, DC, February 2022.

———. "Task Force on Cyber Deterrence." Washington, DC, February 23, 2017.

US Department of Justice. *The False Claims Act: A Primer.* Washington, DC, April 2011. https://www.justice.gov/sites/default/files/civil/legacy/2011/04/22/C-FRAUDS_FCA_Primer.pdf.

US Director of National Intelligence. "U.S. National Intelligence: An Overview." Washington, DC, 2013.

US Government. "Department Federal Procurement Data System: Next Generation." https://www.fpds.gov/fpdsng_cms/index.php/en/.

US Presidency. "Executive Order 9024 Establishing the War Production Board." Washington, DC: American Presidency Project, January 16, 1942. https://www.presidency.ucsb.edu/documents/executive-order-9024-establishing-the-war-production-board.

———. "Preparation, Submission and Execution of the Budget." Washington, DC: White House, July 2020.

———. "A Quest for Excellence: Report of the President's Blue Ribbon Commission on Defense Management." Washington, DC: Packard Commission, June 1986.

Van Puyvelde, Damien. *Outsourcing US Intelligence: Contractors and Government Accountability*. Glasgow: Edinburgh University Press, 2019.

Vinci, Anthony. "The Coming Revolution in Intelligence Affairs." *Foreign Affairs* (September–October 2010).

Voelz, Glenn I. *Managing the Private Spies: The Use of Commercial Augmentation for Intelligence Operations*. Seattle: Create Space, 2006.

Voss, Nathan, and James Ryseff. *Comparing the Organizational Cultures of the Department of Defense and Silicon Valley*. Santa Monica: RAND, 2022.

Weinig, William J. "Other Transaction Authority: Saints or Sinner for Defense Acquisitions?" *Defense Acquisition Research Journal* 26, no. 2 (April 2019): 106–127.

Weiter, Tim. "We Are Lost in the Woods on Acquisition Reform." *Defense News*, May 6, 2021.

Yannuzzi, Rick. "In-Q-Tel: A New Partnership Between the CIA and the Private Sector." Washington, DC: Defense Intelligence Journal, 2000.

You Ji, Jou. "China: Traditions, Institutions, and Effectiveness." In Thomas C. Bruneau and Aurel Croissant, eds., *Civil-Military Relations: Control and Effectiveness Across Regimes*. Boulder: Lynne Rienner, 2019.

Zegart, Amy B. *Flawed by Design: The Evolution of the CIA, JCS, and NSC*. Stanford: Stanford University Press, 1999.

———. *Spying Blind: The CIA, the FBI, and the Origins of 9/11*. Princeton: Princeton University Press, 2007.

Zegart, Amy B., and Kevin Childs. "The Divide Between Silicon Valley and Washington Is a National Security Threat." *The Atlantic*, December 13, 2018.

Index

A-76 Process, 27, 30 (note 30), 33, 134
Abu Ghraib, 66
Accountability, 10, 17 (note 34), 62, 105, 136
Acquisition Innovation Research Center, 140
Acquisition process, 3, 46, 92, 140
Acquisition reform; also, acquisition reform effort, 3, 15 (note 10), 98 (note 33)
Adaptive Acquisition Framework, 28
Afghanistan, 1, 31, 33, 39, 40, 43, 45, 51, 52, 134, 138
Africa, 23, 39, 51, 108, 138
Armed Services Procurement Act of 1947, 25
Armed Services Procurement Regulation of 1960, 26
Artificial intelligence, 88, 108
Authorities, 2, 6, 14, 68, 102, 104, 110, 111, 133, 135

Barnard, Chester, 11, 120
Blackwater USA, 35, 40, 49

CARES Act, 106, 111

Carroll, Lewis, *Alice's Adventures in Wonderland*, 138
Carter, Ash, 2, 3, 9, 28, 89, 101, 102, 133, 136, 137
Center for a New American Security (CNAS), 10, 19
Center for Security and International Studies (CSIS), 7, 34
Central Intelligence Agency (CIA), 64, 74, 75, 91
China, 13, 82, 84, 85, 86, 87, 89, 93, 103, 113, 140
Civil-military relations, 1, 2, 4, 80, 86, 133
Code of Federal Regulations, 2
Cold War, 26, 65, 75, 93, 135
Commercial Operations and Support Savings Initiative (COSSI), 117, 118
Commission on Wartime Contracting in Iraq and Afghanistan, 31, 32 38, 43, 50, 52, 101, 137
Competition in Contracting Act (CICA) of 1984, 70
Competitive bid process, 20, 22, 24, 25

Compliance-centered approach (to outsourcing), 92
Conan Doyle, Sir Arthur, *The Adventure of Silver Blaze*, 61
Congressional Research Service (CRS), 4, 6
Consortia Management, 107
Contingency contracting, 33, 35, 37, 43, 44, 45, 52, 61, 67
Contract, 1, 2, 7
Contracting officer, 4, 11, 13, 14, 45, 46, 120, 131, 135
Contracting officer representative, 48, 49
Convoy security, 40
Core contractor personnel, 68
Covert action, 73
Covid-19, 106, 107, 108, 123
Cyber, 87, 88, 108
Cyber Command, 2010, 87
Cybersecurity Maturity Model Certification (CMMC), 87
Cyberspace Solarium Commission, 87

Defense Acquisition University (DAU), 47, 112
Defense Advanced Research Projects Agency (DARPA), 107, 113, 114, 115, 116, 121, 129
Defense Federal Acquisition Regulation (DFARS), 2, 7
Defense Innovation Unit (DIU), 101, 102, 103, 140
Defense Policy Board, x
Defense Production Act, 25
Defense Science Board, "Fulfillment of Urgent Operational Needs," 90
Defense transformation, 39
Department of State (DoS), 32, 39

Digital Gallium Arsenide Microprocessors, 114, 115, 116
Director of National Intelligence (DNI), 63, 67, 74
Diversity, 69, 72, 75
DoD FAR Supplement, 2
DoD Inspector General, 32, 136
Dunn, Richard L., 93, 112, 114

Emerging military technologies, 87, 88, 89
Emerging Technology Consortium (ETC), 107
Enablers, 65, 109, 110
Expeditionary contracting, 46

False Claims Act of 1863, 21
Federal Acquisition Institute, 120
Federal Acquisition Regulation (FAR), 2, 7, 19, 27, 70, 71, 91, 120
Federal Bureau of Investigation (FBI), 66
Federal pay cap, 11, 122
Federal Procurement Data System (FPDS), 8
Flournoy, Michele A., 113
Fox, J. Ronald, 15 (note 10), 121

Gansler Commission Report, 45, 46
Gates, Robert M., 41
Gazelle, 115, 116
Global war on terrorism (GWOT), 12, 13, 14, 31, 61, 65
Goldwater-Nichols Defense Reorganization Act of 1986, 41
Government Accountability Office (GAO), 3, 4, 88, 123, 140 (note 13)
Great power competition (GPC), 12, 13, 14, 82, 83, 86, 108, 135

Greenwalt, Bill, 125 (note 13), 140

Haines, Avril, 108
Hicks, Kathleen, 108
High risk (GAO evaluation), 3, 19, 51, 61
House Oversight and Government Reform Committee, 49, 72
House Permanent Select Committee on Intelligence, 72, 109

IBM Center for the Business of Government, 10
In-Q-Tel, 70, 71, 91, 92, 101, 108, 136
Incentive, 2, 11, 14, 109, 113, 110, 120, 121, 122, 124
Industry (the "industry"; i.e., contracting firms), 2, 27, 31, 104, 111, 112, 119; as economic and political actors, 10, 11, 14, 51, 52, 91, 120, 121, 137, 140
Innovation, 7, 28, 137, 139
Intelligence community (IC), 9, 61, 63, 64, 65, 66, 67, 92, 108, 109
Intelligence Reform and Terrorism Prevention Act of 2004 (IRTPA), 73, 74
Intelligence services, 63
Iraq, 31, 33, 34, 35, 36, 41, 42, 44, 46, 448, 50, 134

KBR, 37, 38

Lend-Lease Act, 23, 24
Logistics Civil Augmentation Program (LOGCAP), 36, 37
Lopes, Crane, 8
Lord, Ellen M., 7, 123

Mattis, James, 42, 83

McCain, John, 101
McCaskill, Claire, 50
McNamara, Robert, 26
Military consulting firms, 35, 36
Military effectiveness, 4, 5, 86, 133
Military provider firms, 35, 36
Military support firms, 35, 36

National Aeronautics and Space Administration (NASA), 104
National Defense Authorization Act (NDAA), 32, 95 (note 9)
National Defense Strategy Commission, 84
National Defense Strategy of 2018, 82, 83, 87, 88, 93
National Intelligence Strategy (NIS), 69
National Security Act of 1947, 25, 65, 74
National security strategy, 4, 13, 41, 69, 82, 83, 85, 87
Need to know, 63
New technologies, 13, 71, 89, 92, 101, 102, 103, 105, 109, 119, 137
Nisour Square, Baghdad, 40
Nongovernmental organization (NGO), 12
North Atlantic Treaty Organization (NATO), 39

Obama, Barack, 2, 93
Office of Management and Budget (OMB), x, 7
Office of Secretary of Defense (OSD), 2, 47, 83, 84, 113
Office of the Director of National Intelligence (ODNI), 74
Olney, Rachel, 103
Operational contract support (OCS), 13, 33, 37, 41, 49

Opportunity costs, 13, 94, 135
Other transaction authority (OTA), 2, 4, 104, 106, 124 (note 4)
Oversight: Contractors, 4, 20, 22, 23, 41, 46, 47, 48, 49; Intelligence, 62, 69, 72, 73, 74; Great power competition, 89, 137; Synonyms for, 122

Packard Commission Report of 1986, 11, 113, 140
Panetta, Jimmy, 10
The People's money, 2, 66, 108
Personal security, 40
Peters, Heidi M., 14 (note 2), 30 (note 30), 104, 105, 122
Prince, Erik, 40, 49
Private sector: Pre-Cold War, 21, 22, 23, 25, 26, 28; Post-Cold War, 70, 86, 88, 89, 110
Private security contractors (PSC), 32, 38, 40, 49, 51, 52, 61, 62
Project on Government Oversight (POGO), 123
Proprietary, 9
Prototype project, 103, 105, 111, 117, 118

Quadrennial Defense Review (QDR), 83

RAND Corporation, 10, 42, 47, 58 (note 59)
Regulatory constraints, 92
Research and Development (R&D), 5, 7, 89, 117
Risk adverse, 11, 113
Roles and missions, 82, 86
Rumsfeld, Donald, 39

Security clearance, 9, 60, 63, 66, 75, 109

Security escorts, 40
Sensitive compartmented information facility (SCIF), 63
Shinseki, Eric, 39
Silicon Valley, 28, 70, 90, 91, 101, 102, 103, 107, 109
Singer, Peter, 35, 36
Snowden, Edward, 66, 134
Sopko, John F., 52, 53, 138
Soviet Union, 65
Special Inspector General for Afghanistan Reconstruction (SIGAR), 50, 52, 53, 137
Special Inspector General for Iraq Reconstruction (SIGIR), 48, 50, 137
Startup, 70, 87, 90, 91, 94, 102, 103, 107, 115, 123
Static security, 40
Strachan, Hew, 42
Strategic Institute FOR Innovation in Government Contracting, 112, 114
Strategy: Meaning of, 3, 4, 69, 70, 81; Absence in GWOT, 31, 41, 42, 43, 53; Nature of in GPC, 82, 83, 84, 87, 93

Technical innovation, 4, 13, 71, 72, 88, 89, 91, 93, 101, 102, 103, 107, 109, 140
Third Offset Strategy, 82

US Agency for International Development (USAID), 32, 39, 50
US Central Command (CENTCOM), 33
US Congress, 72, 73, 83

Van Puyvelde, Damien, 64, 65, 66, 67, 68, 70

Venture capital, 71, 102, 115, 119

War production board, 23, 25
Webb, Jim, 50
White book, 81
Willy-nilly, 41

Xi, Jinping, 86, 140

Yeshiva, 136

Zegart, Amy, 74, 102, 108

About the Book

EVERY YEAR, THE US DEPARTMENT OF DEFENSE ALLOCATES MORE than $400 billion to for-profit firms. Which raises the question: Where does the money go? Thomas Bruneau takes a deep dive into the murky waters of national defense outsourcing to answer that question. Moving beyond the issue of private military contractors, Bruneau investigates the scope, legality, and implications of the private sector's vast involvement in securing the nation.

Thomas C. Bruneau is distinguished professor emeritus of national security affairs at the Naval Postgraduate School.